SINCLAIR MCKAY

BLETCHLEY PARK

THE SECRET ARCHIVES

PRODUCED IN ASSOCIATION WITH BLETCHLEY PARK

BLETCHLEY PARK

THE SECRET ARCHIVES

PRODUCED IN ASSOCIATION WITH BLETCHLEY PARK

SINCLAIR MCKAY

Aurum
Press

BLETCHLEYPARK

Contents

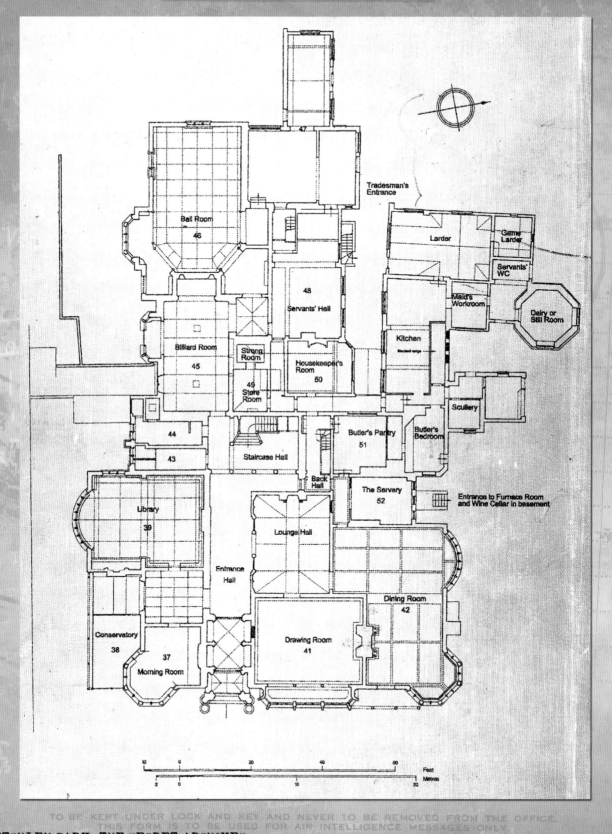

Introduction

IF YOU DID NOT KNOW ANYTHING OF ITS PURPOSE, YOU WOULD NOT SPARE A GLANCE FOR THE ESTATE OF BLETCHLEY PARK IN BUCKINGHAMSHIRE. SIMPLY TO LOOK AT, THE BIG HOUSE – AND ITS GROUNDS AND THE TWO-STOREY CONCRETE BLOCKS AND THE WOODEN HUTS ALL SCATTERED AROUND THE LAKE – ARE THE VERY DEFINITION OF UNREMARKABLE. THE SECRET NERVE CENTRE OF WORLD WAR TWO HAD TO BE BASED SOMEWHERE ANONYMOUS. THE ESTABLISHMENT THAT WAS TO HOST THE MOST RADICAL, BRILLIANT INTELLECTS OF A GENERATION NEEDED A LOCATION SO UNDISTINGUISHED AND FORGETTABLE THAT IT WOULD NEVER ATTRACT THE ATTENTION OF NAZI SPIES OR OF LUFTWAFFE PILOTS OVERHEAD. WHEN SENIOR DIGNITARIES VISITED THE SITE, THEY WERE URGED TO DO SO IN CIVILIAN CLOTHES; TO TURN UP IN FULL MILITARY DRESS WOULD ALERT ANY OBSERVERS TO THE HIGH IMPORTANCE OF THIS INSTITUTION.

During those war years, all that the local Bletchley townspeople knew was that the big house – formerly the home of a wealthy stockbroker turned squire – was now being used for government work. They could hardly not know this: many of the young people working at the Park were billeted in their houses. Beyond that, though, they knew nothing.

Even for those who were recruited to this establishment, and who arrived at Bletchley railway station for the first time, that sense of muffled secrecy continued until after they had got past the military sentry box at the gates of the Park, then walked along the handsome avenue of elms, entered the big house, had their induction talk and signed the Official Secrets Act. When they had sworn their silence, they were told why they had been summoned. This went for everyone: the young undergraduates, pulled away from their studies at the smarter universities; the aristocratic society girls, set on doing their bit in any way they could; the

ABOVE The hermetic atmosphere led to a great many friendships being forged – and romances too.

OPPOSITE A plan of Bletchley's Park's ground-floor. Before the huts were built, everything, including the telephone exchange, teleprinter machines, cafeteria and the codebreakers, crammed into these rooms.

expert linguists; the retired classics masters; the cryptic-crossword-inclined Wrens; the chess champions; and also the young soldiers drawn away from the fields of conflict, pulled back home in order to fight that war with the power of their vaulting intellects. Only after they had pledged to keep quiet – the penalty for transgression was never quite made clear, but many recruits assumed that if they said anything, they would be shot – was the meaning of this strange house on the edge of an unmemorable provincial town in the middle of rather flat countryside pocked with quarries made clear to them.

These days, it is very well known that Bletchley Park was the home to the British code-breaking effort during World War Two. It is common knowledge that here cryptologists pulled off the near unthinkable feat of cracking the German Enigma codes. The work that was done here had a huge, almost unquantifiable impact on the course of the conflict. Whether listening in on the lethal U-boat wolf-packs; analysing the supply lines of Rommel's panzer divisions in the North African desert; helping to hunt down and sink the Bismarck; feeding the Germans disinformation and then monitoring the responses that resulted in V-weapons being given incorrect co-ordinates and falling short of their central London targets; even intercepting and decoding invaluable messages from the inner sanctum of German High Command in the run up to and aftermath of the Normandy landings, the codebreakers seized an invaluable advantage: a means of penetrating deep into the heart of German strategy and tactical thinking. All this without the Germans suspecting that their 'unbreakable' code systems had been laid bare. It is equally well understood that Bletchley Park played host to a fusion of intellectual and engineering expertise that heralded the dawn of the computer age. But during the war – and for many years and decades afterwards – such things were known only by a very few people. For a very long time, the work of Bletchley Park and the dazzling achievements pulled off by its recruits were hidden deep in the shadows; a mass of dark matter in the histories of World War Two. Those who had worked there were obliged to keep quiet for decades afterwards about what they had done. One reason for this was that a great many countries after the war were still using versions of the coding technology that these brilliant people had secretly cracked. And as the silence continued, the fortunes of the big house – an eccentric construction that in some ways mirrored the capricious and colourful personalities who had gathered to work there in the war years – waned. It found diverse new uses, largely for technical training in telephony, but its fabric was beginning to disintegrate.

In the mid-1970s, the first narrow beam of light was shone on the Bletchley secret by one of its veterans, Captain Frederick Winterbotham, in his book The Ultra Secret. Ultra was the

term used for all intelligence that had been gleaned from the successfully broken Enigma codes. Many veterans were shocked that he had chosen to break his vows; the Official Secrets Act was meant to bind one for life. Yet this book was followed, cautiously, by other mentions of Bletchley in intelligence histories. By 1981, there was just enough information for the young novelist Ian McEwan to write a BBC play called The Imitation Game, about a young woman in a World War Two codebreaking centre. More veterans' memoirs followed; but just at the point when the name of Bletchley Park was attaining some sort of familiarity, the old house and the Park itself were facing the prospect of complete demolition and rebuilding. A site of vast — almost immeasurable — historical significance was within a whisker of being transformed into a shopping mall with a modern housing estate attached.

This book is the story both of a house and of an institution. The codebreaking establishment was regarded at the time by some locals as a special kind of lunatic asylum. In some ways, they might have had a point. Bletchley, a modest town engaged in the modest industry of brick-making, and standing on a railway junction linking London with Scotland, and Oxford with Cambridge, had never before seen such a curious and diverse range of residents. Yet there had also been some colour and variety when the house was first bought by Sir Herbert Leon in the late 19th century; he and his wife Lady Fanny brought with them an enthusiasm for riding, a passion for horticulture and hothouses, and an enthusiasm for travel which saw them return from European tours with new ideas for titivating the appearance of the house. A few of Bletchley's wartime recruits were architects by training, and they shuddered with distaste at the exuberant mismatch of styles — an awkward cupola copper dome here, some quasi-Tudor timbering there, and an interior flourish of what one codebreaker described as 'lavatory gothic'.

For some recruits, the house and the neighbouring town were very unsophisticated and primitive. For others, though, hailing from less grand upbringings, the estate had the feel of a fine university campus. And the work that was done here was carried out with similar collegiate ethos; an intoxicating blend of mad energy and discipline and even a radical absence of hierarchy. In certain

departments of Bletchley Park, everyone had a voice, and every suggestion would be taken seriously. From the most experienced of senior codebreakers to the youngest of the Women's Royal Navy volunteers operating the complex machinery, this was an establishment in which each individual contribution mattered enormously.

Given the intense security at Bletchley Park, and the post-war determination that many of its traces be erased, it is quite remarkable just how much photographic material has survived. Not merely contemporary shots of the big house, or of the extemporised wooden huts in which so many of those eureka leaps were made — but also a wealth of images of revolutionary, proto-computing technology, such as Alan Turing's bombe

BELOW Before Bletchley Park and the War, the Government Code and Cypher School was based in 55 Broadway, St James' Park. Prior to the move, one idea was to house codebreakers in dormitories.

machines, or Max Newman and Tommy Flowers' Colossus machines. Now, it has to be said that there were also a number of unauthorised photographs taken at the time: shots of Wrens and codebreakers, working machines or hunched over desks, or simply lying outside on the lawn by the lake, soaking up some sunshine. These pictures were taken for the most innocent of reasons: young people wanting some memento of this dizzyingly intense period of their lives. Now they are utterly fascinating records of a crucial point in history – but back then, those images could have got their owners into trouble. They might have been regarded by the authorities as misjudgements that in the wrong hands could have inadvertently given away vital information. Of course, they did no such thing – and that is what makes the photos here such a delight to pore over. It is as if we are all now being fully allowed in on this secret.

The photographs are valuable for another reason too. Because of the mathematical and technical nature of the codebreaking operation, we tend to hold mental images of Bletchley Park as a rather austere place of spartan work rooms, mind-boggling machinery and serious young people, faces drawn with the effort and the pressure of the work that they were doing. The photographs tell a subtler, warmer and in many ways much more enthusiastic story. Away from the plainness of the huts, there is another life. Codebreakers found many ingenious ways to throw off the weight of their jobs: they formed theatre companies, they played boisterous games of rounders and tennis, they skated during the deep freezes of those cold wartime winters. The photographs also enable us to see unexpected sides to famous names. Given the tragic nature of his premature death in the 1950s, it is extraordinary and rather moving now to look at photographs of Alan Turing in 1939 and beforehand; they serve as a glimpse not only of an inherent cheerfulness, but also of just how

young he was when he made those astonishing mathematical breakthroughs at the Park. Youth also figures large in the images of Wrens, smiling and laughing in the summer sunshine, recovering from all-night shifts tending to mighty, mysterious machinery, but with their thoughts very much on the dances to come with American soldiers.

The photographs also allow us to gaze with some wonder upon the technology that grew out of Bletchley Park. This is a wire-filled world, a world where the use of valves was considered revolutionary. Decades before the first microchip, here is machinery specifically designed to take on tasks that would fry the human brain. We now live in an age when very few of us would know how to reconfigure the insides of our computers. These photographs enable us to wonder at some length what it must have been like, in the middle of a dark, silent night shift, to attend to a proto-computer reaching up to ceiling height which constantly broke down and had to be adjusted with pliers.

In those faces of the young Wrens and code-breakers – those admirably serious and nicely composed head shots that were standard then – we also see something of the determination and pride that enabled them to work with such vigour. Underneath all of this seems to run a seam of good humour which in such an establishment was absolutely vital.

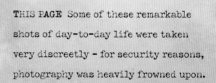

THIS PAGE Some of these remarkable shots of day-to-day life were taken very discreetly – for security reasons, photography was heavily frowned upon.

TO BE KEPT UNDER LOCK AND KEY AND NEVER TO BE REMOVED FROM THE OFFICE. THIS FORM IS TO BE USED FOR AIR INTELLIGENCE MESSAGES ONLY.

10   BLETCHLEY PARK: THE SECRET ARCHIVES

LEFT The 1937 sales particulars; note not only the 'pleasure grounds' but also the enticement of 'factory sites' by the railway.

ABOVE Situated between Oxford and Cambridge, with London just 50 minutes away by train, Bletchley Park was perfectly positioned for the first wave of recruits.

Within these images there is a valuable sense of context: from the blackout tape on windows, to the ordinary streets of terraced houses in which codebreakers would have moments of blinding insight into Enigma, or where exotic figures such as the writer Angus Wilson would disconcert his landlords with his very metropolitan habits and dress sense. You occasionally have to remind yourself that this was all just seventy-five years ago or so. In some ways, it feels and looks further away than that. Even more splendidly antique now, though, are the wonderful images of the house when it belonged to Sir Herbert Leon and Lady Fanny. Here really is a lost world: grand weekend parties, lavish hunt balls, stables and gardens, innumerable servants gathered together for group shots, and the Edwardian elegance of the lady of the house herself. Even from its earliest days, the life of Bletchley Park was one of sometimes unconventional fizz and energy.

Then there are the images of the fall and rise; the slow melancholic decline of the house throughout the post-war years and then its brilliant and heartening rescue by the Bletchley Park Trust, and the glorious restoration work which is still proceeding apace. The house of Bletchley Park is – by the standards of most historical properties – a stripling, having only stood for around 130 years. Yet it has seen and played host to more extraordinary feats and achievements than a great many far older stately homes. The codebreakers have granted it a form of immortality. The words 'Bletchley Park' are now synonymous the world over with British genius. The eccentricity of the estate and of the codebreaking establishment are here captured in a wealth of images that help to recreate a perfectly unique point in history.

The Lake, Bletchley Park

THE HOUSE AND GROUNDS

1

LEFT Bletchley Park had a beautiful cricket pitch, plus an elegant pavilion that mirrored the architecture of the main house. It was sold before the war; the pitch was later used by Bletchley Grammar School.

A FEW YEARS AGO, THE TELEVISION SERIES *ANTIQUES ROADSHOW* FEATURED A COUPLE OF EDITIONS FILMED IN FRONT OF THE MANSION OF BLETCHLEY PARK. WERE IT NOT FOR THE ILLUSTRIOUS WARTIME HISTORY OF THE HOUSE, IT IS EXTREMELY UNLIKELY THAT IT WOULD HAVE DONE SO. INDEED, IT IS QUESTIONABLE WHETHER THE HOUSE WOULD HAVE BEEN THERE AT ALL, OR WHETHER IT WOULD HAVE BEEN CHEERFULLY DEMOLISHED WITH LITTLE IN THE WAY OF AESTHETIC REGRET. THE HOUSE ITSELF DOES HAVE A FEW ADMIRERS; BUT ITS MANY DETRACTORS OVER THE YEARS HAVE HAD THE BETTER LINES. HOWEVER, THE HOUSE AND THE SITE ARE ACTUALLY FASCINATING IN THEIR OWN RIGHT, AND THE ESTATE IS A BEGUILING SNAPSHOT OF A MOMENT OF SOCIAL HISTORY.

It is thought that some sort of house – though obviously not the present one – has stood on the site of Bletchley Park since the medieval period. Ownership of the land seesawed between various families, and various houses were built and then came down. Especially notable was an 18th-century Palladian effort erected by the antiquarian Browne Willis. By this stage, the land around had been imparked, then turned back to purely agricultural use, and then imparked again. It is possible, though we will never know, that the Browne Willis incarnation of the property was the most aesthetically pleasing by a very long way. But ownership switched again and in 1805 that house was demolished and practically nothing remains in terms of records.

Throughout much of the 19th century, the site was most probably occupied by a farmhouse, lived in by a Mr Coleman. But the mansion that we see today was most probably started (again, the records are not conclusively clear) by Samuel Seckham, a businessman, surveyor and architect. This was at some point in the 1870s, when the little village of Bletchley would have been greatly expanded, thanks to the railway and the works that came with

it. The locale could never really have been described as a prime beauty spot.

As well as designing this new house, at first an unassuming construction of red brick and black slate, Seckham also remodelled the gardens and the fields around, landscaping them with lakes, and also avenues of trees that would help to muffle the clanking and shrill whistle screams from the railway lines, which some have suggested he found wearing. There were also lines of limes and elms, but not long after the house was built, he decided to sell up

PREVIOUS PAGES Bletchley Park had a beautiful cricket pitch, plus an elegant pavilion that mirrored the architecture of the main house. It was sold before the war; the pitch was later used by Bletchley Grammar School.

OPPOSITE When the popular BBC television series Antiques Roadshow filmed editions at Bletchley, the crowds and the queues were prodigious.

and move elsewhere in the county. Owing to its favourable proximity to London, he probably knew that he would have no difficulty finding a buyer. The grounds and the property were then bought by Sir Herbert Leon in 1883, and it was he who decided to add to Seckham's original.

Sir Herbert was a successful stockbroker who went on to become very active in politics; first sitting on Buckinghamshire council and then, in 1891, getting himself elected as Liberal MP for Buckingham. David Lloyd George was a frequent visitor to the house. Sir Herbert was then defeated in 1895, but his energies found other outlets, and he helped with an organisation called the Rationalist Free Press. With Bletchley Park, he took what was rather an ordinary Victorian house and, whatever one might think of the end result, it was

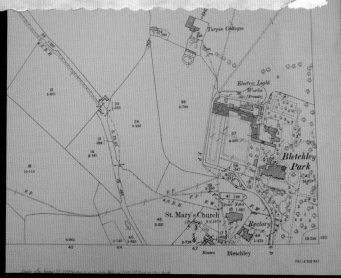

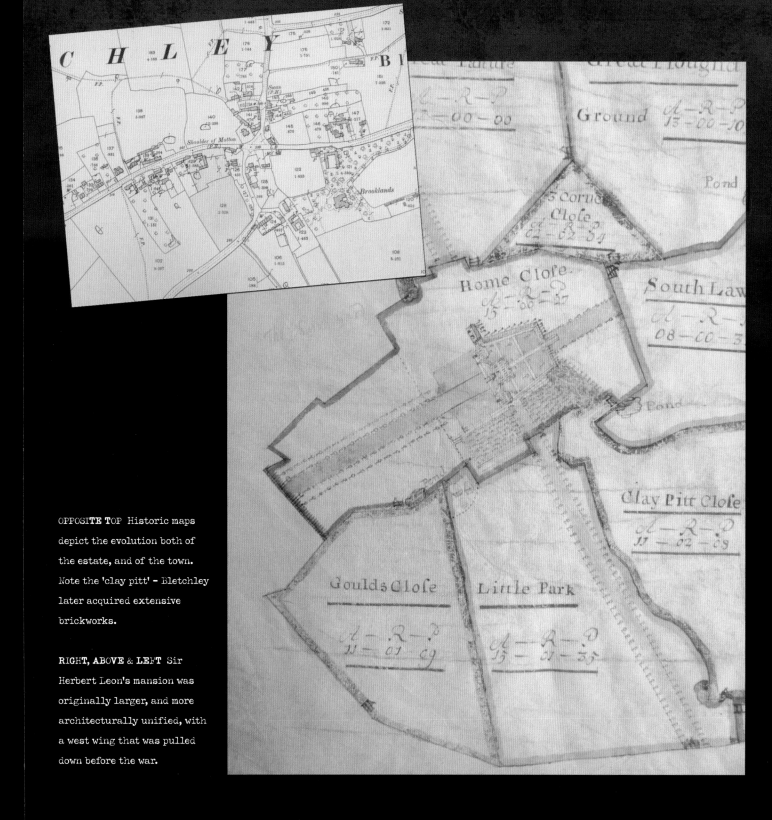

OPPOSITE TOP Historic maps depict the evolution both of the estate, and of the town. Note the 'clay pitt' – Bletchley later acquired extensive brickworks.

RIGHT, ABOVE & LEFT Sir Herbert Leon's mansion was originally larger, and more architecturally unified, with a west wing that was pulled down before the war.

LEFT Sir Herbert Leon: parliamentarian, wealthy stockbroker and enthusiastic squire, who played an energetic role in the life of the local community.

RIGHT Lady Fanny Leon, who presided over the estate's busy social diary: the grand balls, the hunts, the whirl of weekend parties. She also involved herself with the local council and nursing association.

SIR HERBERT AND LADY FANNY LEON

SIR HERBERT WAS MARRIED TWICE; HIS FIRST WIFE DIED IN 1875. HE THEN MET FANNY HIGHAM AND A COUPLE OF YEARS LATER, THEY WED. BLETCHLEY PARK WAS NOT THEIR ONLY HOME – THEY ALSO HAD PROPERTIES ON THE KENT COAST, AND UP NEAR BALMORAL IN THE HIGHLANDS OF SCOTLAND. BUT BLETCHLEY WAS THE REAL FOCUS OF THEIR PRIVATE AND SOCIAL LIVES (THE HOUSE FREQUENTLY RECEIVED HIGHLY DISTINGUISHED VISITORS, INCLUDING DAVID LLOYD-GEORGE). THE LEONS' COMMITMENT TO THE COMMUNITY STILL ECHOES TODAY: IN 1970, THE LEON SCHOOL AND SPORTS COLLEGE WAS CONSTRUCTED ON THE BLETCHLEY LAKES ESTATE. MORE RECENTLY, IT TRANSMUTED INTO THE SIR HERBERT LEON ACADEMY. IT IS HEARTENING THAT DESPITE ALL THAT HAPPENED HERE, WHEN IT COMES TO LOCAL HISTORY, THE CODEBREAKERS DO NOT HAVE A COMPLETE MONOPOLY.

certainly less ordinary afterwards. His builders used the same kind of brick and slate but Sir Herbert had much grander plans involving a ballroom, a library, an extensive still-house for cold storage of dairy products, a proper suite for his wife Lady Fanny, and quarters for servants.

These days, the eye is drawn to the copper cupola which seems rather awkwardly jammed on to one side of the house's roof. Sir Herbert's taste was eclectic, and is reflected in the contemporary dark wooden panelling, the occasional outbreaks of stained glass and the ornately plastered ballroom ceiling which the Hon. Sarah Baring said made her think of 'drooping bosoms'. Apologists for the structure say that any prejudice against it is a manifestation of anti-Victorian sentiment, a dislike for the pre-modern, and that its merits will be seen properly in time. Whether that is the case or not, the Bletchley Park Trust is doing a terrific job in restoring it to its original glory.

This was more than just a family home; this was a house built for entertainment, and for weekend parties. The addition of

TO BE KEPT UNDER LOCK AND KEY AND NEVER TO BE REMOVED FROM THE OFFICE
THIS FORM IS TO BE USED FOR AIR INTELLIGENCE MESSAGES ONLY.

18   BLETCHLEY PARK: THE SECRET ARCHIVES

FROM LEFT TO RIGHT The estate cricket team; the rather splendid horse and trap, ready to convey guests and luggage from the station.

BELOW Making the most of some scarce time off, the household staff gather together in their smartest array.

The Lake, Bletchley Park

extensive stables to the side were there for those who wanted to ride out into the countryside; equally, the yew tree maze and the lawns flanking the lake were there for more sedate promenades. The lake itself was supposed to have dated back hundreds of years, when it was in use as a medieval fishpond. In its new life, it became the home of noisy geese. In later years, some of Bletchley's younger female recruits recalled being harassed by the geese as they attempted to take coffee by the water. These water features also resulted in an abundance of frogs, which were recalled with a shudder by one young Wren who dreaded the walk back through the estate at the end of a shift at midnight, in the blackout, and inadvertently treading on frogs in the darkness.

The estate had other delicate touches, such as the beautifully tended orchid house, the extensive rose garden and the kitchen garden. The Leons employed huge numbers of local people and

TOP An Edwardian picture postcard, hand-coloured. Note the tower at the rear of the house: it had been pulled down by the time the codebreakers arrived.

ABOVE The estate's gardeners assembled. Their work ranged from tending rare orchids in the hot-houses to cultivating the kitchen gardens – which were later to contribute much needed fresh produce to the codebreakers' canteen.

RIGHT Lady Leon rode out with the Whaddon Hunt; and the sheer numbers of Bletchley Park's stable staff illustrate the importance of hunting to the estate.

BELOW A memento of the 1891 election in which Sir Herbert became Bletchley's local member of parliament. This was at a time when the vote was very restricted – how many in this picture would have been entitled to cast a ballot?

POLLING DAY MAY, 1891

RIGHT The estate's agricultural fairs were always popular, both with farmers, and with visitors from around the county. Firework displays were also a draw.

their in-house staff, according to the census of 1891, numbered 200 – everyone from personal maids to blacksmiths. More than this: Sir Herbert and Lady Fanny had intended the house to stand as a sort of focus for the local community, and as the years wore on, they used the grounds for agricultural fairs, horse shows and firework displays. They were popular too; a few Bletchley locals recalled how they were particularly assiduous at arranging and paying for care for the sick and the elderly, and how Sir Herbert donated playing fields and recreation grounds.

In 1926, Sir Herbert, who had been made a baronet in 1911, died; it is said that this was the only time that the church bells of Bletchley were stopped from ringing. Sir Herbert had found their noise intensely irritating, but the local vicar had ignored all his requests to tone them down a little. On the occasion of his passing, however, it was felt that he might at least have that one comfort.

For a few years afterwards, his widow continued to live at the house but when she died, the couple's son, Sir George Leon, made the decision to sell the estate off. In 1938, it was bought up by Captain Hubert Faulkner, who was heading up a consortium of property speculators. There was a suggestion that he and his colleagues had plans to demolish and rebuild. However, these plans were almost immediately frozen by the intervention of the Foreign Office, and Admiral Sir Hugh Sinclair. The house was acquired; the Admiral, to make up for bureaucratic slowness and stinginess, is said to have paid for the house out of his own pocket.

Immediately it was pressed into service. Up in the far reaches of the house, near the old water tank, is a tiny room that once had enormous significance; for this was 'Station X'. The Fleming-esque designation actually had a mundane meaning – Station 10. It was a wireless listening post, and the complicated aerial was arranged around the Wellingtonia tree outside the window. Not long after

BELOW Quite apart from the gardens and stables, Sir Herbert and Lady Fanny employed large numbers of domestic staff for the house. The work was constant, but the Park was regarded as a good situation.

RIGHT A 1930s glimpse of the extent of the Bletchley stables; by the time Alan Turing started work in adjacent offices, they had been cleared.

BELOW The courtyard is still there today, near the entrance of the building termed 'the Cottage', where senior codebreaker Dillwyn Knox worked.

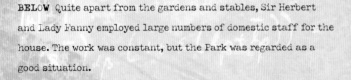

TO BE KEPT UNDER LOCK AND KEY AND NEVER TO BE REMOVED FROM THE OFFICE. THIS FORM IS TO BE USED FOR AIR INTELLIGENCE MESSAGES ONLY

22   **BLETCHLEY PARK: THE SECRET ARCHIVES**

this came Captain Ridley's Shooting Party; far from being one of Sir Herbert's weekend entertainments, this was in effect the dress rehearsal for the Government Code and Cypher School to make the move from London and into the English countryside, a much less likely target for bombing than the streets around Whitehall and St James's Park.

By the summer of 1939, the preparations for the move were almost complete; but it is now instructive to think of this from the point of view of all those Bletchley locals. Once a focal point for the town's communal life, Bletchley Park was now instead a secret establishment. Questions about its use would not be answered. These local people would have been looking on as the rolls of barbed wire around the external fencing went up. In the space of a few years, the estate had gone from being a benevolent local employer and benefactor to a place about which you were not encouraged to speculate. In time, as the war started, these local people would of course have all sorts of outsiders billeted upon them. To some, the change cannot have been completely welcome.

One of the Park's senior figures, Nigel de Grey, wrote a rather wistful account about this stage in the life of the house. 'There is no moment in time more beautiful than the first days of a fine autumn such as were the last days of August 1939 and the last days of peace … in such richly romantic atmospheric conditions, even the architectural vagaries of Bletchley Park were wrapped in a false mellowness and almost but never quite achieved the appearance of a stately home.' This might have been the view of the grand de Grey, a fastidious gentleman who had been a senior figure in an auction house and who sometimes favoured a cloak. But as the Park's work expanded, and the numbers grew, there were a number of young people for whom this place would have seemed as grand and gracious as Brideshead itself. And the place still clearly harboured echoes of happier memories. A little later on, Nigel de Grey wrote to a friend in Cairo who was clearly familiar with the old place from before the war. 'You would not recognise your old country seat of 1938. All kinds of new buildings appear on the spacious grounds on which you used to gambol.'

But what would Sir Herbert and Lady Fanny have thought? It's easy to imagine that they would have been thrilled that the house had found such a vital use. Ruth Sebag-Montefiore was a friend of the family who – as it happened – was also one of the very first

to be recruited to work there. She recalled in her memoirs the house in happier times, with those weekend parties and people itching to go off riding. Yet didn't the house in its new incarnation draw precisely the sort of people that the Leons would have found fascinating, from their near-neighbour Alfred Dillwyn Knox, whose brother had been the editor of Punch, to the swarms of girls in pearls, to visits from Lord Louis Mountbatten, and of course Winston Churchill himself? Would they not have been thrilled that Brigadier Tiltman's first office in the house was in the old nursery, and still had Peter Rabbit wallpaper? Or that the first teleprinters were installed at the back near the ballroom? Or that the first dining room was presided over by a chef drafted in

from the Ritz? Would the Leons not have been beside themselves with pleasure to see the ballroom being used so extensively by so many bright young things? Even their tennis court went on to see a remarkable amount of use in the summer months.

For many grand country properties around the country during the war, government requisition was often no joke; the carelessness of countless troops caused all sorts of havoc and dilapidation. But Bletchley Park took on a life that somehow seemed perfectly in keeping. Like the man who built this rather eccentric house, the codebreakers who came to work there were similarly unpredictable, madly enthusiastic and sometimes lacking in what many would regard as normal taste.

LOSS OF MESS TRAPS.

The breakage and loss of tea cups knives and forks, and other mess taking place on a fantastic scal

The rate of loss is no less tha that n—...lly experienced in a

...and plates hav ...rubberies ...roken.

Tumb
pus
of

AFTERNOON TEA.

Owing to the time now being taken in collecting afternoon teas, arrangements are being made to obtain a limited number of tea urns which will be supplied to Heads of the larger Sections so that they can make their own arrangements, if and as desired, for the serving of tea in their huts.

These urns have a capacity of about 70 cups.

2. Tea (in kind) would be available for collection in bulk over a week at 10 a.m. on Mondays from the Cafeteria and milk daily from the Cafeteria at 2 p.m. in exchange for tea tickets @ 1d. per head. The present allowance of tea is 1 lb. for 200 persons and 2 pint of milk for 10 persons.

3. Will Heads of Sections who may desire to adopt the above procedure please let me know not later than noon on Tuesday next, 26th May, stating the average numbers of persons for whom tea is required.

4. For those who do not wish to make use of this scheme, tea (already made) will continue to be available for collection from the Recreation Hut daily between 3.15 and 4.15 p.m.

2

Conversion to Codebreaking Factory

PREVIOUS PAGES A marvellously rare pre-war aerial shot of the estate: note the fine yew maze on the right, which had to be grubbed up to make way for huts.

ABOVE Linguists work through decrypts late into the night, as indicated by the presence of the heavy blackout on the window in the background. In the foreground, an inactive Enigma machine lies open.

OPPOSITE Young ladies operating Typex machines; long shifts working on endless chaotic jumbles of letters required dogged patience and much dedication.

LARGE THOUGH THE MANSION OF BLETCHLEY PARK IS, IT WAS IMMEDIATELY APPARENT TO THE DIRECTOR, COMMANDER DENNISTON, THAT MORE SPACE WAS GOING TO BE REQUIRED. THE VERY HEART OF THE PARK WOULD HAVE TO BE CONVERTED. AND IT IS THIS BLETCHLEY PARK THAT WE STILL SEE TODAY. THE SIGHT OF THE HUTS HAS A PECULIARLY STRONG RESONANCE; THESE APPARENTLY MAKESHIFT, RATHER DOUGHTY STRUCTURES STRONGLY CONVEY THE SPIRIT OF THE WAR EFFORT. IT IS VERY EASY TO IMAGINE HOW UNCOMFORTABLE THEY COULD BE TO WORK IN: BITTER DRAUGHTS WHISTLING THROUGH IN THE WINTER MONTHS, AND THE STIFLING AIRLESSNESS OF HIGH SUMMER. THEY ALSO PROVIDE A POWERFUL VISUAL EXAMPLE OF THE ACUTE NATURE OF THE WORK. THOSE WHO WORKED IN HUT 4 JUST BY THE SOUTH SIDE OF THE HOUSE WOULD HAVE HAD NO IDEA ABOUT THE WORK BEING CARRIED OUT IN HUT 1, ON THE HOUSE'S OPPOSITE SIDE.

Fittingly, the apparent anarchy of the codebreaking ethos was reflected in the way that the first of these wooden huts, and their functions and numbering, were decided in the autumn of 1939. In other words, they were extemporised – and then adapted to the different needs of different parts of the operation. For instance, Hut 1, it is thought, was originally intended as a radio transmission/ reception station. It was built just to the north of the mansion. But how was it that Hut 2 immediately became known as 'the beer hut' and served this purpose pretty much throughout the War, serving strong refreshment to codebreakers, debutantes and Wrens alike? The atmosphere of Hut 2 was so reliably convivial that often it was almost impossible to move down the central corridor, so packed was it with people.

The military section of the operation was initially allocated Hut 3. The original inhabitants of Hut 4 are lost to time; it went on to be occupied by codebreakers focusing on naval encryptions. These days, it is occupied by hungry visitors to Bletchley Park eager to sit down for a cup of tea and a Cornish pasty. Hut 5, meanwhile,

as well as being first allocated to the naval section, had a most intriguing addition: a sunray parlour. This was not a luxury tanning booth, but a vital means for those who worked long hours in windowless rooms – such as the WAAF teleprinter operators – to try and grab a semblance of sunlight, and to keep up their vitamin D levels.

Hut 6 was one of the earliest to find a wider fame, for it featured in the title of Gordon Welchman's 1982 memoir of the Park's work. It was intended to deal with army and air force Enigma messages. These would be brought in in great bundles from

listening stations around the country – for instance, motorbike couriers would race up from Chatham, Kent, through the night to deliver batches of freshly intercepted messages. Welchman himself counselled his readers not to pay too close attention to the numbering of huts, as it would all be too confusing in the end.

It seems that Alastair Denniston's broad idea was to have all these huts arranged around the house in a sort of star shape, the better to ease communications between them and the directorate. Yet they seem to have ended up being dotted around the grounds of the house in a slightly more random fashion. Part of this was to do with plumbing, for of course these structures had to have conveniences. Also, there were other considerations, such as machinery. Hut 7, for instance, was built some distance away from all the others because it housed heavy tabulating contraptions; the noise from these devices would have been an intolerable distraction for codebreakers in other sections.

It seems fair to say that the most famous of the huts is Hut 8, and this is thanks in part to the presence of Alan Turing, and the radiator to which he kept his tea-mug padlocked when he wasn't using it. It was in this hut that some of the tensest weeks and months of the entire war were played out. Turing and his team had triumphed brilliantly in cracking the Naval Enigmas. But in 1942, Admiral Dönitz had a feeling that he needed to be more careful; and he was responsible for adding a fourth rotor to the Naval Enigma machines. This created countless more potential encryption combinations and it brought Hut 8 to a standstill for about six terrible months. Huts 3, 6 and 8 were all huddled together, and though those within were fastidious about keeping their work quiet, there was a great deal of practical inter-hut communication.

There were other outposts; the fine yew maze was grubbed up to make way for Hut 10, which dealt with low-grade coded messages – those that weren't encrypted via the Enigma machine. Then, as well as the beverages on offer in Hut 2, there sprang up a NAAFI kiosk, which sold everything from chocolate to stockings to cigarettes (rationing permitting). Veterans recall how when the kiosk shutters went up, codebreakers came running out of their various huts and started to queue, as though they were children waiting eagerly by an ice-cream van.

But as the War progressed, so too did the work of Bletchley; what had started out as an improvised, establishment, making it up as it went along, was now getting bigger and sleeker. And the more brilliant the results that it delivered, the more was demanded of it by the War Office. By 1942, the codebreakers were reading and translating and analysing countless thousands of messages from every theatre of war around the world. While Hugh Alexander and his team in Hut 8 were focusing on the war in the oceans, increasing numbers of recruits were being given crash courses in Japanese language, history and culture in order to help them crowbar their way into the fearsomely complex Japanese codes.

The huts were now joined by rather more permanent-looking structures (with greatly improved lavatorial facilities). These concrete buildings, designed to withstand bomb blasts, and positioned close to the ever-expanding teleprinter sections, were simply called 'the Blocks'. Block A was on two floors – naval cryptography on the first floor, military on the ground. It was soon joined by Blocks B and C. The term utilitarian hardly does them justice; they were blank, pale and low. These buildings gave no hint whatsoever of the type of work that was being carried out within. But if they were less friendly-looking, they were also much more comfortable. By this stage, about 9,000 women and men were working shifts at Bletchley Park; the volume of material being produced was staggering. The work and the numbers could not have been accommodated in ever-proliferating wooden huts.

There were other crucial additions too, including a sickbay, to which a number of Wrens had to be sent – the job of operating the bombe machines, with their noise and their fiddly complexity, had induced minor nervous breakdowns in some. One operative recalled how the work – a demanding task combined with a frazzling 24-hour rota system – got the better of her at one stage. She was ordered to spend a couple of days in bed in the sickbay with a jug of water by her side. This she did and, remarkably, it did her the power of good. She got back to work straight away. There was also the crucial addition of a cafeteria. In the first days of the establishment, meals were served and taken in the dining room of the house, and there was waitress service. The cafeteria

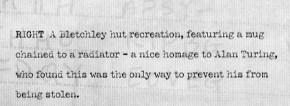

RIGHT A Bletchley hut recreation, featuring a mug chained to a radiator – a nice homage to Alan Turing, who found this was the only way to prevent his from being stolen.

FAR RIGHT The telephone switchboard for Hut 8, which at the height of the Battle of the Atlantic was Bletchley's nerve centre. Parts from such switchboards were appropriated by brilliant GPO engineer Tommy Flowers and became elements in the world's first computer.

BELOW A cross-section of life in the different blocks and huts, including (above left) the intercept control room in Hut 6 and (bottom left) the information collation point in the same hut. Despite the advent of new technology, the work was still reliant on pencil, paper and human focus.

brought with it a distinctively American-style innovation: self-service.

It also came to symbolise another important aspect of life at the Park and that was the apparent lack of fixed hierarchy. Bletchley veterans who had been among the younger codebreakers recalled how, after a gruelling all-night shift, one could go for breakfast and find oneself sitting next to a colonel on one side, and an American major on the other, with no sense that lower ranks had to take themselves elsewhere. All mingled as equals; and faced the equally daunting prospect of Woolton pies (a rationing invention which involved dispensing with the meat element and adding in a great many root vegetables), tarts that tasted of 'cardboard' and the very occasional meal where a salad came inadvertently garnished with some dead insects. The cafeteria staff were also very sharp and strict about portion control. One young lady, having had her main course, slipped on a pair of sunglasses and went back to the counter to try and get

another helping, pretending to be someone else. Her ruse was spotted. On other occasions, American codebreakers looked on with wonder at one of the finest British archetypes. 'They must have their tea, of course,' noted American cryptographer William Friedman, 'at 10.30 and 4.30.'

Tea was a continual sore point, if BP internal memos are anything to judge by. It was felt by the directorate at one stage that rather too much time was spent in the fetching and drinking of it. To this end, huts were provided with their own urns, which had the capacity for '70 cups'. But this in turn provided fresh aggravation for the canteen, which prompted another cross internal memo concerning losses and breakages of crockery. These, said the memo writer, would appear to be worse than those suffered on a man o'war. The implication was that the messy disorganised academics could not even be entrusted with teacups. And they couldn't. Some discarded cups were found in hedges .

Block C was possibly the noisiest of all the Bletchley sections; from 1943, this is where the Hollerith machines operated. These involved a card-punch system and had actually been eveloped for

the retail world. But, rather like Alan Turing's bombe machines, they proved adept at checking through vast quantities of information very quickly. Blocks D, E and F were to follow, and Block F was to hold its own special historical significance: the site where the computer age might be said to have properly dawned.

The departments run by Professor Max Newman (the 'Newmanry') and Major Tester (the 'Testery') were in Block F, and it was here, later in the war, that the new German 'Fish' or 'Tunny' codes were broken. It was also here that the Colossus machine made its debut: the combined brainchild of Turing, Newman and the GPO's Dr Tommy Flowers, Colossus was a super-fast machine working on revolutionary valve technology that could run through immense quantities of information. It was thanks to Colossus, and the efforts of the Newmanry, that encoded messages were read not merely from German High Command, but from Hitler's office itself.

Added to all this in the grounds were garages (for the numerous drivers and motorcycle couriers), plus Nissen huts for the military police. For any of the Bletchley locals who had been familiar with these grounds from the Leon family's annual summer fete, the sight of the blocks through the fencing would have looked quasi-industrial, as well as futuristic. There was something in the deliberate featurelessness of these buildings that oddly reflected the impersonality of the machine age. It is perhaps fitting that in the years immediately following the war, these blocks continued to be used by the most secretive of all Britain's secret services: GCHQ (Government Communications Headquarters). Their purpose was as a training centre for new recruits.

Throughout all of this, Bletchley Park's directorate confined itself to the first floor of the main house, where Nigel de Grey's office looked out directly on to the lake. It was into the main house that each new recruit was sent

upon arrival, in order to be greeted by Commander Travis, and to sign the Official Secrets Act. While part of the ground floor of the house had been converted in the early months of the war for purposes so secret that even the codebreakers were not to know (such as photographic development rooms, and a special annex for the 'teleprinter princesses', as the WAAFs who did this work were known), by the early 1940s it would not have been unusual for any codebreaker to wander in through the house to hear the strains of 'By the Sleepy Lagoon' (also used as the theme tune for Radio 4's Desert Island Discs) echoing out from the ballroom, as the dancing enthusiasts trod a lively lunchtime step.

Yet within the house some incredibly grave work continued. Brigadier Tiltman, who had an astounding aptitude for levering his way into all sorts of different codes, from Russian to Japanese, also worked alongside Oliver Strachey at one stage on receiving decrypts from Germany's railway system. The men worked not in a hut but in one of the upstairs rooms. And so it was that, with horror, they were able to read regular reports of the numbers of men, women and children being taken to concentration camps and of numbers of 'discharges' from these camps. Brigadier Tiltman's room was the nursery – the one still decorated with the Peter Rabbit wallpaper. At other points throughout his Bletchley career, it was noted that Tiltman did not like to work sitting down, and had a special desk constructed that would allow him to work

RIGHT In sparse surrounds, and on a 24-hour rota, linguists would translate decrypted German messages into English. The poster is an exhortation to save fuel.

standing up. And even though he had his own proud military rank, any other codebreakers nipping into the house to see him were treated with startling informality; one young recruit, in uniform, introduced himself by walking into the brigadier's office and stamping his heels with a salute. The brigadier looked down at the young man's army issue boots and said: 'I say, is it really necessary for you to be wearing those?'

Keeping the house's secretarial staff in order was a fierce but fair PA called Doris Reid, who worked for Nigel de Grey. While the young girls who worked for her went in fear – Miss Reid was extremely rigorous in all things, from grammar to general behaviour – they also came to love her as 'a true diamond'. Miss Reid, in her main house office, was at the administrative heart of Bletchley, succeeding in bringing a semblance of order to such matters as canteen vouchers and requests for leave.

In the early years, veterans recalled the establishment having at least something of the atmosphere of a country house, in the sense of its looseness and lack of formality. When Winston Churchill was to pay his visit in 1941, he would have looked out over a great muddle of wooden huts (with Huts 3 and 6 connected by means of a small wooden tunnel, through which documents could be pushed on a tea-tray, by means of a broom handle). Given the awesome dimensions of the concrete Admiralty Citadel on Horseguard's Parade, he must have been a little beguiled by the seeming untidiness and randomness of these higgledy-piggledy huts around the house. The later blocks spoke perhaps of a more professional approach. They certainly pointed to a future in which the art of codebreaking would become a highly processed science.

BELOW An exasperated memo from the directorate concerning losses and breakages of tea crockery – note the draconian measure of instituting canteen 'watchmen'.

BELOW Some of the American codebreakers admired the ritual British devotion to tea, but the authorities were annoyed by the amount of time each break took.

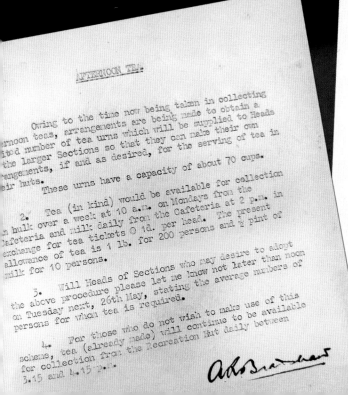

AFTERNOON TEA.

Owing to the time now being taken in collecting afternoon teas, arrangements are being made to obtain a limited number of tea urns which will be supplied to Heads of the larger Sections so that they can make their own arrangements, if and as desired, for the serving of tea in their huts.

These urns have a capacity of about 70 cups.

2. Tea (in kind) would be available for collection in bulk over a week at 10 a.m. on Mondays from the Cafeteria and milk daily from the Cafeteria at 2 p.m. in exchange for tea tickets @ 1d. per head. The present allowance of tea is 1 lb. for 200 persons and ½ pint of milk for 10 persons.

3. Will Heads of Sections who may desire to adopt the above procedure please let me know not later than noon on Tuesday next, 26th May, stating the average numbers of persons for whom tea is required.

4. For those who do not wish to make use of this scheme, tea (already made) will continue to be available for collection from the Recreation Hut daily between 3.15 and 4.15 p.m.

A.D. Bradshaw

LOSS OF MESS TRAPS.

The breakage and loss of tea cups, tumblers, knives and forks, and other mess traps is taking place on a fantastic scale.

The rate of loss is no less than five times that normally experienced in a man-o-war.

Tumblers, cups and plates have been found pushed away into shrubberies and left about office, many of them broken.

This state of affairs cannot be allowed to go on and it has become necessary to prohibit the removal of any Government property whatsoever from the dining rooms except by members of the kitchen and dining room staff. The watchmen have orders to stop anyone carrying Government crockery, etc. away from the dining rooms and to take their names. Those who wish to have milk in their offices must provide their own gear.

RIGHT From the lake,
a 1939 glimpse both of
the house and (right) the
newly built Hut 6, where
the German Army and Air
Force codes were to be
cracked.

The Cryptologists

THE ECCENTRIC, ANARCHIC WARTIME BOFFIN HAS BECOME A BRITISH ARCHETYPE, AND THE BLETCHLEY PARK STORY IS WHERE IT FINDS ITS HIGHEST EXPRESSION. WE HEAR IT IN MAVIS BATEY'S (NÉE LEVER) AFFECTIONATE ACCOUNT OF HER MENTOR, THE VETERAN CODEBREAKER ALFRED DILLWYN KNOX; WHEN DEEP IN THOUGHT, HE WOULD OCCASIONALLY TRY TO REFILL HIS PIPE WITH SANDWICHES. HE WAS ALSO, APPARENTLY, INCAPABLE OF FINDING THE RIGHT DOOR OUT OF THE ROOM ON THE FIRST GO, HEADING AT FULL TILT INTO STORE CUPBOARDS.

'Dilly' Knox (born in 1884) was a Cambridge classicist who had smashed codes during the Great War in Whitehall's Room 40; very often inspiration would come in a bath that he had found in an office at the end of a corridor. He thought best in hot water. On one occasion, worried colleagues had to force open the door to check that he hadn't drowned. He was engrossed in calculations.

In the inter-war years, Knox worked with the Government Code and Cypher School, partly on Soviet encryptions, but also devising ways of defeating early versions of Enigma, which had been brought into use by Germany and also Spain. An expert on ancient papyri, Knox was fond of testing his female recruits to Bletchley with lateral teasers. 'Which way round do the hands of a clock go?' was one. The answer: it depends whether one is observing the clock or whether one is the clock itself. Such posers

LEFT Alfred Dillwyn 'Dilly' Knox, photographed and sketched. A classicist who once challenged Sir Arthur Conan Doyle over the details of a Holmes story, he had a firework temper, which he always directed towards his immediate superiors.

were intended as mental exercises to help when confronting intractable coding difficulties; to inculcate the habit of approaching insoluble problems from wholly unexpected angles.

Knox was 55 years old at the outbreak of World War Two and from the start of Bletchley's work, there was a sense that his rigorous, time-consuming methods were being superseded by developing technology. Nevertheless, he was a force to be reckoned with, on and off duty. He was a terrifying driver, especially along country lanes; he was given to reciting Milton, and gesticulating along with the verse, his hands off the steering wheel. He also had a marked preference for working with young, attractive (and tall) women. The obvious reasons aside, there has been some suggestion that this is also because he found that women like Mavis Lever had exactly the right mental approach towards the exhausting work. In 1941, aged 20, Miss Lever was

OPPOSITE (from front to back) Alan Turing, Robert Augenfeld, Karl (surname unknown) and Fred Clayton. In February 1939, Turing and his friend Clayton sponsored two Jewish refugee boys from Vienna – Turing paid for Augenfeld's education. They were in Bosham, West Sussex in August 1939 just days before Turing reported to Bletchley Park for duty.

LEFT Mavis Lever (later Batey), who worked closely with Dilly as a 20-year-old from the University of London. He taught her how to crack codes by hand – a system using a form of slide-rule, known as 'rodding'.

responsible for cracking the Italian Enigma codes that led to British victory in the Battle of Cape Matapan.

Knox was matched in eccentricity by another codebreaking veteran, Joshua (Josh) Cooper, a large good-humoured Oxford classicist and linguist (an expert in Russian), known to some as 'the bear', who would inadvertently frighten new young recruits by suddenly shouting apparently random phrases, such as 'Yes, that's it!' But Cooper's aide, Ann Cunningham, felt moved to proclaim in later years that incidents such as the time when he threw a coffee cup into the lake because he could not think what to do with it were isolated. Although the idea that it happened just once is still beguiling.

It should also be borne in mind that Cooper's work in the Air Section against the Luftwaffe led to his cryptology career continuing long after the war at GCHQ. Cooper understood very well the impact that the coming computer age would have and was adept at communicating this to younger colleagues. His occasional outbreaks of falling under desks, or re-starting conversations with people weeks later at exactly the point that they had left off previously, helped to camouflage the intense seriousness with which he took his work.

The cumulative effect of stories such as these is to help us find a frame for their unimaginably complex achievements. Yet there are other dimensions to their great innovations. Professor Max Newman, before he was recruited to Bletchley Park, had lectured Alan Turing at Cambridge, and had overseen his revolutionary paper 'On Computable Numbers' – a 1936 work meshing far-sighted mathematics and philosophy that heralded the coming of the computer age. Seven years

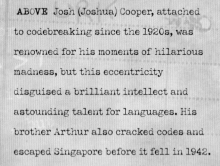

ABOVE Josh (Joshua) Cooper, attached to codebreaking since the 1920s, was renowned for his moments of hilarious madness, but this eccentricity disguised a brilliant intellect and astounding talent for languages. His brother Arthur also cracked codes and escaped Singapore before it fell in 1942.

LEFT Young codebreakers relaxing at lunchtime – and looking for all the world like undergraduates – watch as the work of building a shelter continues.

RIGHT Professor Max Newman was a visionary mathematician who foresaw the spread of computers – and worked with Alan Turing and Tommy Flowers to bring that age into being. An expert pianist, with a sly wit, he was adored by those who worked in 'the Newmanry'.

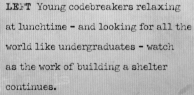

NIGEL DE GREY

IN 1915, AS THE THUNDEROUS BOOMS OF CONFLICT ECHOED ACROSS FROM FRANCE AND BELGIUM, 29 YEAR OLD NIGEL DE GREY, AN OLD ETONIAN SERVING WITH THE ROYAL NAVAL AIR SERVICE, WAS TRANSFERRED TO NAVAL INTELLIGENCE AND JOINED A DEPARTMENT KNOWN AS ROOM 40. IT WAS NAMED SIMPLY AFTER THE SPACE IT OCCUPIED IN THE ADMIRALTY BUILDING ON HORSEGUARDS PARADE. HERE WERE GATHERED THE CODEBREAKERS – INCLUDING ALISTAIR DENNISTON AND ALFRED DILLWYN KNOX – WHO WOULD LATER BECOME ARCHITECTS OF BLETCHLEY TRIUMPHS. IN WWI, THEY WORKED ON CODEBOOKS CAPTURED FROM GERMAN SHIPS AND ZEPPELINS. AND THE EXPANDING TECHNOLOGY OF WIRELESS BROUGHT A PROFUSION OF INTERCEPTS, GATHERED AT HUNSTANTON IN NORFOLK. IN 1917, DE GREY DECIPHERED A KEY DIPLOMATIC TEXT WHICH BECAME KNOWN AS THE ZIMMERMAN TELEGRAM (SEE P 127); IT BROUGHT THE US INTO THE WAR. THERE WAS ALSO ROMANCE IN ROOM 40: OLIVE RODDAM, A CLASSICIST FROM KINGS COLLEGE CAMBRIDGE, FELL FOR DILLY KNOX.

to encapsulate the near-anarchic ethos of Bletchley Park's greatest hours. As well as being arguably the finest mathematical genius of his generation, Turing was a prodigious runner, and is said to have once run along the Grand Union Canal from Bletchley all the way back to London, 48 miles away. This is to say nothing of his later adoption of a ginger cat that would – unusually – accompany him on country walks. And then of course there was the matter of his sexuality. Turing was gay at a time when homosexual acts were illegal, and punishable with a prison sentence. Turing's eventual fate – prosecution for 'gross indecency', subsequent 'chemical castration' and loss of his security clearance – was far worse. He committed suicide in June 1954. But his time at Bletchley was touched with triumph.

When he joined in 1938, he was just 26 years old. Together with Gordon Welchman, Turing took the principle of the Polish 'bomba' code-checking machines, developed in the 1930s by three brilliant Polish mathematicians, and turned them into the 'bombes' – vast wardrobe-sized machines (of which more in chapter five) that could run through thousands of coding combinations far faster than any number of humans. Turing went on to head up Hut 8, devoted to the problem of breaking into the Naval Enigma. This he and his team eventually did – but they hit a period of disaster when Admiral Dönitz made the decision to increase security and added a fourth rotor to the Enigma machines. Later in the war, when squaring up to the advanced technology of the German 'Lorenz' codes, Turing came a step closer to bringing the programmable computer to life with his contribution to Colossus.

The art and science of cryptography saw a swerve in emphasis as wartime recruitment stepped up; mathematicians, previously regarded as temperamentally unsuitable, were now actively sought out, rather than the previous World War One preference for classicists. One young man, John Herivel, found a crucial way into the Red Luftwaffe codes aged just 21. Another prodigy was Oxford-educated grammar school boy Peter Twinn. He made the

later, Professor Newman was in his department, 'the Newmanry', working both with his apt pupil Turing and also engineering genius Dr Tommy Flowers on the Colossus machine – an electronic leap forward that would enable Bletchley to crack the more advanced German 'Tunny' codes. Newman was remembered not for eccentricity, but for genuine egalitarianism; 'the Newmanry' was renowned for its meetings where everyone could pitch in with codebreaking ideas, and also suggestions about how the department might be run more agreeably.

In recent years, some Bletchley veterans have felt that the tragedy of Alan Turing has crowded out the achievements of the Park's other luminaries. Yet Turing's story somehow seems

SOME OF BLETCHLEY'S MOST INSPIRED MINDS:

Rolf Noskwith

Jack Good

Frank Birch

John Herivel

Peter Twinn

Harry Hinsley

Leslie Yoxall

first successful Enigma codebreak of the war – the cracking of an old Wehrmacht message that nonetheless gave his team some leverage into the current day-to-day codes. There has been a suggestion that Turing nursed a small crush for Twinn, and indeed on one occasion asked him if he would like to go to bed. The request was politely declined, but the fact remains that Turing was remarkably open about himself, and was not shunned as a result. Bletchley recruits were more tolerant than the wider world outside.

Hugh Foss was another of the Park's great minds, an expert on Japanese encryption. Initially recruited to the Government Code and Cypher School in 1924 on account of his unusual ability with that language (he was born in Kobe to a missionary father), he always cut a distinctive figure. Foss stood six foot five, with a red beard and a taste for wearing sandals. As the war progressed, he was put in charge of the Japanese naval section in Hut 7; veteran Wren Molly Morgan recalled that in the rare quiet periods he

would relax by solving crosswords in Russian. In off-duty hours, he would also seek to relieve the intense pressure of work in spectacular displays of elegant Scottish Highland dancing. It was through this activity that young codebreaker Oliver Lawn was to meet his future wife, the linguist Sheila MacKenzie. Foss was very intense about organisation, even insisting at home that the washing-up had to be done in a very particular order, with saucers coming first.

Slightly more grounded was Gordon Welchman, a senior mathematics lecturer at Cambridge, who distinguished himself at Bletchley with remarkable innovations (he added the 'diagonal board' to Turing's ideas for the bombe machine, which greatly increased its efficacy).
He was also the boffin instrumental in turning this febrile semi-detached institution into something more resembling a super-sleek efficient factory. It was his technocratic powers of organisation that made possible a system whereby countless thousands of

encrypted messages, sent in from every part of the world, would be filtered through 24-hour-a-day departments, decoded, analysed, filed, and then sent upwards through the pyramid system to the War Office and then Churchill himself. Even now, the prospect is extraordinary; so many different departments, concentrating on so many different theatres of war, and decrypting and processing at prodigious speed all messages, both significant and mundane. It was Welchman who turned Bletchley into this most inspirational of factories.

One slightly left-field codebreaker who could have been a full-time mathematician had it not been for his devotion to chess was the young and (according to many smitten women) very good-looking Hugh Alexander. Before the war, he taught at Winchester – but he won increasingly prestigious prizes at chess, and his superlative skill in that area made him an ideal Bletchley recruit. He was Alan Turing's deputy in Hut 8, before the impractical Turing was eased out and deployed more effectively elsewhere; Alexander took over and made it a model of efficiency and speed. He was brilliant both at theory and application, but also, rather more rarely, ensuring that his colleagues remained completely

LEFT Though at first glance it looks as if he is relaxing, this rare shot captures Alan Turing deep in study. Veterans recall that he was often abstracted, and that even mundane social greetings would make him look panicked.

motivated and pepped with enthusiasm. This quality saw him transferred later in the war to HMS Anderson in Colombo, leading a Far East codebreaking team. Indeed, so good was Alexander in what to him must have been an unexpected field that after the war he was lured back into it to join the newly formed GCHQ establishment in Cheltenham. He did so, and excelled there. Even when he got to retirement age, they could not bear to let him go. He stayed another couple of years and even after that the Americans tried to recruit him. Yet Alexander's abiding passion throughout was chess; he wrote books on the subject and – even as his cryptography career continued – columns about chess for various newspapers.

Even the more driven of the senior codebreakers had surprising hinterlands. While senior cryptologist

BELOW Today's Bletchley Park museum has a fascinatingly detailed recreation of Alan Turing's Hut 8 office, right down to pencil stubs and tea mug (chained to radiator!)

LEFT While at Cambridge in the 1930s, Turing bought himself a teddy and named it Porgy. He practised his complex mathematical lectures out loud before it; Porgy was an attentive listener.

Frank Birch was quite an office politician within Bletchley Park, staunchly demanding that he and his Naval Enigma team should have more time allocated to them with the bombe machines, outside codebreaking his interests were startlingly eclectic. Not only was he an actor and theatre producer who had essayed a warmly received Widow Twankey at the London Palladium, he was also a historian whose most substantial published work was a book about racehorses. Similarly, the Park's original director Alastair Denniston had passions other than codes; as a young man he was a gifted athlete who had taken part in the 1908 Olympics.

There is no doubt that the free-thinking ethos of Bletchley, with what Commander Denniston termed its 'professor types', was a source of terrific friction in intelligence departments higher up. See it from their point of view: an establishment with what seemed the loosest of hierarchies, and filled with young people like Turing who appeared to have the greatest difficulty explaining themselves to anyone not on their intellectual plane. The pressure to get a crowbar into the Naval Enigma codes – with the Battle of the Atlantic raging and Britain in grave danger of having all its supply lines cut off – could not have been greater. It is easy to imagine senior figures in Whitehall being fearful that the abstract geniuses of Bletchley might simply be too otherworldly to have

any kind of success.

Yet it was thanks to that intellectual vortex, that theoretical free-for-all, that the greatest leaps were made. Hut 6 codebreaker Keith Batey pointed out that you needed a particularly detached frame of mind to do the job effectively, commenting that one would hardly expect someone to solve a cryptic crossword with a gun being pointed at their head. For all that Alan Turing cycled through the countryside wearing a gas mask; for all the fantastical shapes thrown by Hugh Foss as he danced Eightsome Reels in the house's ballroom; and for all of Dilly Knox's endless capacity for writing acidly rude memos about his superiors, and his textbook mad-professor irascibility, and his apparent ability to subsist entirely on chocolate and coffee, this was the atmosphere that worked for them. There was a genuine freedom to experiment, to think, to enquire. The Honourable Sarah Baring, a naval card index recruit, repeated with feeling the sentiment that in the absence of any

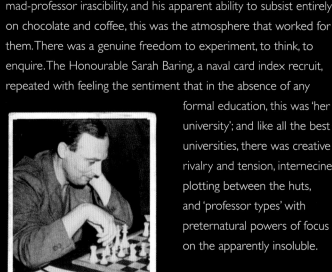

formal education, this was 'her university'; and like all the best universities, there was creative rivalry and tension, internecine plotting between the huts, and 'professor types' with preternatural powers of focus on the apparently insoluble.

ABOVE Codebreaker Hugh Alexander was obsessed by chess; female codebreakers, by contrast, were obsessed with him and his 'dazzling blue eyes'. In the 1950s, he played – and won – chess contests against Soviet grandmasters.

LEFT Senior codebreaker Frank Birch (second from left) on his graduation day from King's College, Cambridge in 1909; Birch had an unusual hinterland as a successful theatre producer, and as a pantomime dame.

BELWO Commander Alastair Denniston created and led the Bletchley operation until 1942.

BOTTOM Commander Denniston goes to the palace to receive his Companion of the Order of St Michael and St George (CMG) in 1941.

TOP & ABOVE Scenes from Denniston family life, with the Denniston children on the lake at Bletchley Park (**ABOVE**).

The Girls, the Pearls and the Musical Sergeants

4

ABOVE Women's Royal Naval volunteers on parade. Having passed stringent intelligence and aptitude tests, thousands were sent to work at Bletchley and its out-stations around the world.

Keep mum she's not so dumb!

CARELESS TALK COSTS LIVES

PATRIOTIC SERVICE
for
BRITISH WOMEN

WOMEN WANTED URGENTLY

to enrol for the duration
of the war in the

W·A·A·C

WOMEN'S · ARMY · AUXILIARY · CORPS
and the

W·R·N·S

WOMEN'S · ROYAL · NAVAL · SERVICE

ENROL TO-DAY

Apply at the nearest **EMPLOYMENT EXCHANGE** for full particulars.
Ask at Post Office for the address.

NATURALLY AN ENTERPRISE AS AMBITIOUS AS BLETCHLEY PARK – WITH ITS AIM TO READ ALL THE MESSAGES AND THUS THE MIND OF THE GERMAN WAR MACHINE – NEEDED MANY MORE PEOPLE THAN JUST TALENTED MATHEMATICIANS. IN 1940, AFTER HAROLD 'DOC' KEEN AND THE BRITISH TABULATING COMPANY HAD DELIVERED THE FIRST OF TURING AND WELCHMAN'S BOMBE MACHINES, IT WAS UNDERSTOOD THAT THESE REVOLUTIONARY BEHEMOTHS WOULD NEED DEDICATED OPERATIVES. SO IT WAS THAT THE FIRST WAVE OF WRNS – WOMEN'S ROYAL NAVY RECRUITS – ARRIVED. THIS INITIALLY SMALL BAND OF YOUNG WOMEN HAD BEEN SELECTED FOR THE JOB BY MEANS OF APTITUDE AND INTELLIGENCE TESTS. SOON, AS THE NUMBER OF MACHINES GREW, SO DID THE NUMBERS OF WRENS, AND THEY WERE BILLETED IN REQUISITIONED STATELY HOMES ALL AROUND THE LOCAL AREA, FROM WOBURN ABBEY TO WAVENDON MANOR. MANY OF THESE YOUNG WOMEN HAD NEVER EVEN LEFT HOME BEFORE. NOW, THEY FOUND THEMSELVES IN DORMITORIES IN HOUSES FILLED WITH OLD MASTERS WHERE, IN CERTAIN SEASONS, THE PARKLAND OUTSIDE WOULD BE FILLED WITH THE NOISE OF RUTTING DEER.

The work was obviously gruelling; as we will see in chapter five the bombes were ingenious at checking through coding combinations at very high speed. But the mechanisms were delicate too, and needed constant maintenance. For Wrens on night shifts, all this fiddling around with fine wires and tweezers added a further level of strain, caused by the need for non-stop concentration over an eight-hour period. On top of which there was the noise and the fine sprays of oil that the machines would give out, making blouse cuffs black. So, in some senses, to get back on the bus and be driven back to your dormitory in the grand house, at whatever time of day and night, must have seemed like sanctuary.

One veteran recalled that it was rather like a girls' boarding school. Another remarked that one inconvenience at Woburn Abbey was a constant lack of hot water, not to mention a lack of facilities for drying. One Wren confessed that a little later in the

OPPOSITE The Womens Royal Naval Service – so central to the success of Bletchley Park – also had a strong role to play at the Service's inception in 1917 during World War One (from when this poster dates).

ABOVE Woburn Abbey – where many of Bletchley's Wrens were billeted – was loved for its opulent scale, but hated for its poor drainage. After the War, the East Front depicted here was demolished.

War, she took to drying her underwear on a rack above the (very hot) Colossus machine.

Because this was the navy, certain aspects of naval discipline and service were rigidly adhered to. Uniforms had to be just so, and the women had to be prepared to parade. But there were quirks in the system too. One veteran Wren recalled how at Bletchley Park, they didn't receive the daily rum ration that was apportioned to all other arms of the navy. To make up for it, they got two pence daily, which, as she said, was very nice as she 'could buy pink gin with it'. This being the time it was, there was a marked element of the glass ceiling about their work; it was generally felt that these Wrens would not be able to cope with anything other than reasonably simple (if intense) tasks. But later in the War, one young codebreaker called Gordon Preston did make an effort to see if the Wrens in his section could at least be told exactly what it was they were doing in mathematical terms, and he approached Professor Max Newman about it.

Newman was later to be one of the Park's most open figures, inviting good ideas from anyone on any level. But initially, it seems, he was very sceptical, proclaiming that the women wouldn't care for the 'intellectual' effort. In the end, however, he was persuaded, and a series of talks for Wrens was advertised. The take-up for these lectures was tremendous. It might not exactly have been parity but at least there was a sense that information wasn't being withheld simply because they could not have understood it.

Preceding the Wrens at Bletchley had been an influx of debutantes. In the earliest days of Bletchley Park, it was initially felt by some at the Foreign Office that women would be better off kept out of it altogether, on the grounds that ladies were notoriously bad at keeping secrets. This stance, which seems hilariously patronising now, was modified a little to allow for rather smart girls, many with titles, to be recruited for the more grindingly routine (yet absolutely vital) work of card indexing. The girls were hooked in via the Establishment social network and came, as one veteran said, from the 'better sort' of families. This is because it was felt they would have more of a sense of duty towards the nation. These antediluvian notions aside, the smart girls were a great asset to the Bletchley operation: enthusiastic, cheerful and quick-witted. The ever-present pearls tended to be tucked inside jumpers, the better to preserve them. Every decrypt would carry with it names, technical terms, geographic references, every single one of which was noted by these young women, using different-coloured pencils, and then inscribed on to index cards under every category. This meant that when terms recurred, intelligence analysts could go back to previous messages. In some cases, this fast-growing index also helped to find ways into some of the Enigma codes, the technical terms being used as 'cribs'.

One other advantage many of these young women brought with them was a familiarity with continental languages, having spent time abroad either finishing their education or on tour. Many of them had, in the mid-1930s, spent a substantial amount of time in Germany and had witnessed at first hand the growing ugliness of the regime, and of the society. Familiarity with that language, as well as Italian, led to a number of these young ladies being hastily recruited to the operation. Background security checks on these girls amounted to being certain that they did not share Mitford-style sympathies towards the Nazi hierarchy.

Most of the girls were largely stoical about the conditions they were presented with in this small, predominantly working-class town; for Sarah Baring, it was a long way from the cocktails that she would enjoy with friends at Claridge's. Her friend Osla Henniker-Major (née Benning) was equally advantageously placed. At one time, she had a romance with Prince Philip, before he became engaged to Princess Elizabeth. At Bletchley, she was teased about becoming a Greek princess. Feet rather more firmly on the ground belonged to Jean Campbell-Harris (now Baroness Trumpington) and Rosamunde Pilcher (who would go on to become a successful novelist). Unlike the Wrens, who were all pitched in together, the card index women were, like the codebreakers, billeted with families around the area. Perhaps there were some allowances made to class sensibilities, for many ended up in agreeably upmarket surroundings – local rectories and manor houses – where they might be expected to find 'their' sort of people.

The Honourable Sarah Baring was grateful for her lodgings, which she shared with Osla and an older codebreaker whom they did not care for. Her only complaint was the cold of the countryside; instead of the roaring fireplace that she might have expected at her family home, her room had a rather sparse electric heater. And that was not sufficient to warm the (seemingly) perpetually freezing air in winter.

No one ever seemed entirely certain whether Bletchley Park was a military or civilian establishment, so there was a blend of uniform and everyday wear. But there were a few soldiers sent to be stationed in a camp just outside the Park. These men preferred the routine of uniform and kit inspections, though even then it was clear that this was no ordinary army camp. There was, for instance, a music tent. This contained a piano, which

TO BE KEPT UNDER LOCK AND KEY AND NEVER TO BE REMOVED FROM THE OFFICE.
THIS FORM IS TO BE USED FOR AIR INTELLIGENCE MESSAGES ONLY

52   BLETCHLEY PARK: THE SECRET ARCHIVES

LEFT A far cry from chilly
billets: Wrens at Woburn Abbey had
the run of rooms like these; also
an impossibly grand lavatory and a
bath, raised on a dais.

on one occasion was being played
beautifully by Corporal Wilfred
Dunwell. The wife of the chairman
of the rural district council was
being shown around the camp by
Ian Mayo-Smith, and she remarked
to him on the sweet music. He explained that Corporal Dunwell
was in fact a professor of piano at one of London's more
prestigious musical academies. Mayo-Smith recalled other musical
colleagues such as Sergeant Herbert Murrill, who also happened
to be director of music at the BBC, and was ideally placed at
Bletchley to keep half an eye on the evacuated BBC Orchestra,
which was stationed a few miles away in Bedford. As we will see
elsewhere, this link between music, mathematics and an aptitude
for cryptology is one that was repeated at all levels throughout
Bletchley Park.

    As well as the Wrens and the regular army, Bletchley also had
its own contingents of Auxiliary Territorial Service (ATS) women
and Women's Air Force (WAAF) recruits too. One ATS, Helen
Currie, arrived a little later in the War and was posted to operate
machinery in the Testery (a department named after its head,
Major Tester). Like everyone else, she found some shifts more
testing than others. But she was also subject to military routine,
and would have to sleep in an army camp. She recalled having to
carry her bedding to a special 'night hut' (a hut set aside for those
who needed to sleep in the day away from noise after a night
shift) in the pouring rain and also piling into the canteen to find
the only choice was 'liver swimming in water'.

    The rigours of a military life at Bletchley were also recalled
by WAAF operatives, called in to work the teleprinters, who also
had rigorously sparse accommodation. They lived in Nissen huts,

THIS PAGE Local Bletchley women also volunteered for work at the
Park. The establishment needed a number of support roles – from
canteen workers to messengers – but the level of intense secrecy
remained the same whatever the work.

and were some distance away either from showers or lavatories.
WAAF veteran Jeanne Isaacs recalled the ordeal on rainy nights or
on bitter winter days of having to scamper across to the notably
un-luxurious ablution block.

    The Park also needed secretarial staff, and messengers too.
Bletchley's youngest recruit was Mimi Galilee, aged 14 when she

first walked through the gates and, in a state of some awe and indeed terror, was directed to sign the Official Secrets Act. Mimi ran messages and packages between all the huts; as a result, she gained an almost uniquely broad overview of the Park, and of who worked where. There were a great many places to which she was not allowed any kind of access; she would knock at a hut door, wait for it to be opened, and hand over the package without getting much of a glimpse inside. She answered to the formidable Miss Reid, and on occasion when her attitude was felt to be wanting, Reid threatened to tell Mimi's mother. Mimi also looked on in some wonder at the advent of the American contingent of codebreakers; at how these smooth and confident chaps seemingly wasted no time finding romance with the women of the Park. There was little that escaped a watchful teenager's eyes.

Later, Mimi graduated to working in the main house, in the suite of offices used by the Bletchley Park directorate. It was there that she worked much closer under the tutelage of Doris Reid. Indeed, many years afterwards, the two women managed to get in touch once more, and Mimi became good friends with the boss she once feared.

The Official Secrets Act also covered staff such as chauffeurs and canteen workers. All these different people and occupations gave the Park not only a distinctly youthful atmosphere, but also one that was not dominated by a single class; for all the Fair Isle-jumpered codebreakers and the debutantes with voices like cut glass, there were also thousands of young women and men drawn from more down to earth backgrounds. The social jumble was found fascinating on all sides: the debutantes beguiled by the energy and confidence of the local girls they saw at the village dances; and the grammar school-educated codebreaking men mesmerised by women who, as one veteran said, they would only otherwise have read about in the upmarket gossip columns of newspapers.

RIGHT Wrens billeted at nearby Wavendon Manor, a handsome 18th century house. According to veteran Molly Morgan, the place was reputed to have the inconvenience of a haunted bathroom.

W.R.N.S. QUARTERS
ADMIRALTY PROPERTY.
PRIVATE.

LEFT & BOTTOM LEFT The intense pressure could induce nervous breakdowns; but many Wrens hailing from industrial towns found the countryside around Bletchley refreshing and conducive to long walks.

ABOVE & TOP Wren Ruth Bourne recalls how she guessed what sort of work she was being drafted in to – she had read enough thrillers, she said, to recognise a codebreaking operation when she saw one.

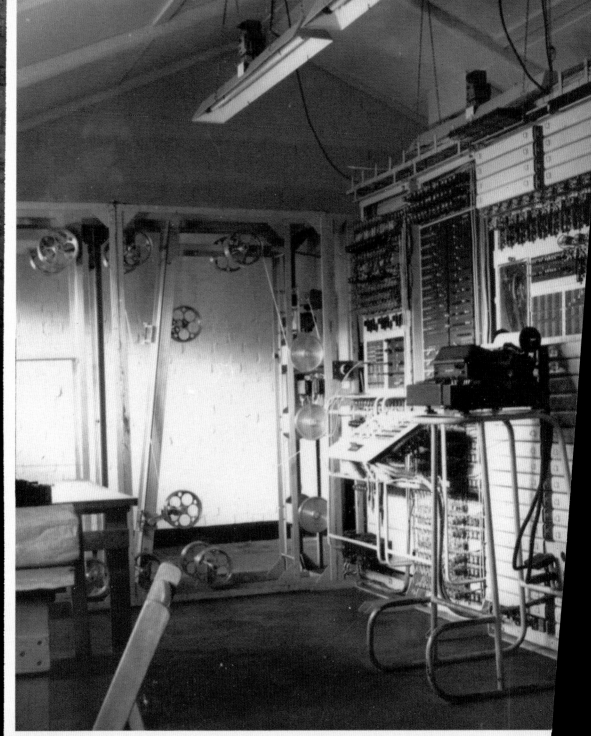

RIGHT   The shape of things
to come: an early Colossus
machine in 1944. It was
set up, wrote codebreaker
Jack Good, by means of
'Boolean plugging and toggle
switches' – in other words,
the forerunner of what was to
become computer programming
language.

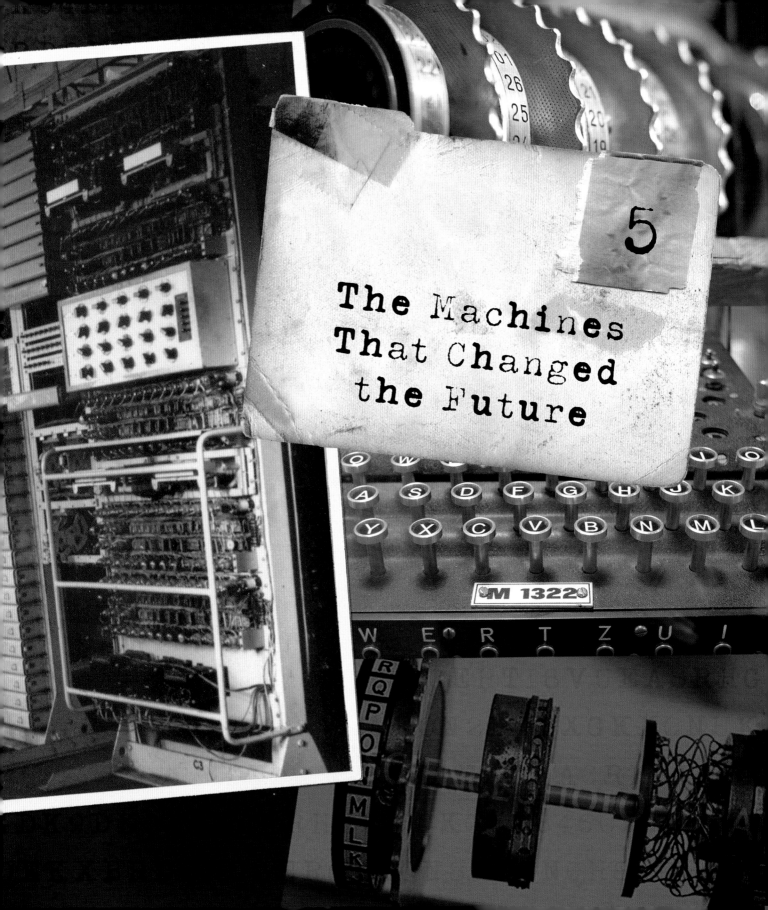

5

The Machines That Changed the Future

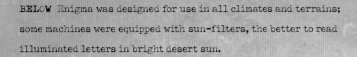

BELOW Enigma was designed for use in all climates and terrains; some machines were equipped with sun-filters, the better to read illuminated letters in bright desert sun.

ABOVE Though the German military had bought up all the exclusive rights to Enigma, they licensed it to a few other territories – notably Switzerland and Hungary.

RIGHT A The four-rotor naval Enigma caused a terrible black-out in Hut 8 for months in 1942; the horrible complexity of the earlier models was multiplied many times over.

FOR A DEVICE DESIGNED TO TAKE LANGUAGE APART AND SCRAMBLE IT INTO IMPENETRABLE CHAOS, THE ENIGMA MACHINE WAS A REMARKABLY NEAT-LOOKING CONSTRUCTION. MADE OF WOOD AND BRASS AND BAKELITE, IT HAD A STANDARD GERMAN KEYBOARD LAYOUT, PLUS A LAMP BOARD WITH LETTERS THAT WERE ILLUMINATED FROM BENEATH, SLOTS FOR MEDAL-SIZED BEVELLED WHEELS AND, DOWN AT ITS FRONT, WHAT LOOKED LIKE A MINIATURE TELEPHONE SWITCHBOARD, WITH SMALL PLUG-HOLES AND TIDY WIRING. IT WAS PERFECTLY PORTABLE; THE MACHINE CAME IN A WOODEN CASE AND COULD BE VERY QUICKLY PACKED UP. IT LOOKED LIKE THE SORT OF MACHINE ONE MIGHT FIND IN AN ACCOUNTING OFFICE, OR EVEN PERHAPS ON A NEWSPAPER EDITORIAL FLOOR, BUT IT WAS DIABOLICAL IN ITS INGENUITY.

Unlike other encoding systems, which might rely on simple letter substitution – an 'X' for an 'A', for instance – every time a key of Enigma was pressed, one of the brass rotor wheels would move, and the 'A' might next time be substituted with a 'Q', lit up on that lamp board. The weakness of letter substitution systems is that the most commonly used letters, such as 'E', might be spotted even in code by means of their frequency in a string of coded letters. The Enigma eliminated that comfort. You could take a simple sentence in plain language and throw it into an infinity of randomness, with

a potential for millions upon millions of letter combinations. This machine was the nightmare challenge faced by the mathematicians of Bletchley Park.

Yet even before the War, there had been extraordinary – and highly secret – successes in attacking it. The Enigma itself was patented in 1918 by Arthur Scherbius. It had been intended as a commercial encryption device; in the mid-1920s, there was a sales brochure to promote it. 'Ciphering and deciphering has been a troublesome art hitherto,' it read, this document aimed at business leaders and financial houses. 'Now we can offer you our machine "Enigma", being a universal remedy for all those inconveniences.'

The sales staff were also quite aware of its potential for military use. In 1926, the British were offered a version. They turned it down. The German Navy, however, decided to pick it up.

ABOVE The Enigma rotors, spindle, and contact wiring; described by BP card index operative Carmen Blacker as 'the most ingenious thing I have ever seen'.

They swiftly made a few alterations to ramp up its security and by the end of that decade, Enigma was being rolled out across what was left of the German military after the Treaty of Versailles. Even as early as 1929, there were those in the Polish government who were sufficiently concerned by this development to try and take precautions against it. Polish intelligence began a trawl for gifted mathematicians and three in particular were to make their name, attaining a sort of cryptological immortality: Jerzy Rozycki, Henryk Zygalski and Marian Rejewski.

It was Rejewski himself who said, 'Wherever there is arbitrariness, there is also a certain regularity. There is no avoiding it.' This sense of mathematical and philosophical openness was to

lead him and his colleagues to some remarkable and invaluable successes. By 1932, they had broken one of the early Enigma systems. And as the decade wore on, with the Germans (and after 1933, the Nazis) working harder on constantly updating and improving the Enigma device, Rejewski and his team, with the help

BELOW Teleprinters were the spine of Bletchley's top secret communications traffic; though in the early days of the War, there were so few that they were situated under the staircase in the mansion. On quiet nights, their operators used to snooze on cardboard boxes.

BELOW The teleprinters clattered out messages from all time-zones day and night; and later in the war, the technology was given its own home in a blast-proof block. By 1945, there were some 400 teleprinters at Bletchley alone.

TELEPRINTER PRINCESSES

'THE NOISE,' ACCORDING TO WAAF CAROLINE SHEARER, 'WAS DEAFENING AND AN UNBELIEVABLE AMOUNT OF PAPER WAS SPEWED OUT.' THE MACHINE THAT DID THE HUGE HEAVY-LIFTING OF THE WORLDWIDE CODEBREAKING OPERATION WAS THE TELEPRINTER. THROUGH THESE MACHINES CAME ENCODED MESSAGES FROM ALL AROUND THE GLOBE. ALTHOUGH THE TECHNOLOGY WAS NOT NEW – VERSIONS OF TELEPRINTERS, WHICH HAD PRINTED OUT MORSE MESSAGES ON A CODED SYSTEM CALLED BAUDOT, HAD BEEN AROUND SINCE THE NINETEENTH CENTURY – THEIR SPEED AND EFFICIENCY WAS AWESOME, AS INDEED WAS THAT OF THE BLETCHLEY WOMEN WHO HAD TO OPERATE THEM. THESE WOMEN, OFTEN DRAWN FROM THE WOMEN'S AUXILIARY AIR FORCE, WERE KNOWN AS THE 'TELE-PRINCESSES' AND WERE LIKELY UNDER THE FIERCEST VOWS OF SECRECY. CAROLINE SHEARER RECALLED HOW, ON ONE OCCASION, SHE WAS OUT IN TOWN WITHOUT HER UNIFORM CAP. WHEN PULLED UP BY AN OFFICER FOR THIS TRANSGRESSION, SHE REFUSED (QUITE RIGHTLY) TO SAY WHERE SHE WORKED. OFFICIAL FURY ONLY ABATED WHEN TELEPHONE CALLS TO HIGHER AUTHORITIES WERE MADE. THE WORK OF RECEIVING AND TRANSMITTING WAS NOT GLAMOROUS; BUT GIVEN THE NEED FOR TOTAL ACCURACY AND FOCUS, IT WAS HUGELY, IF QUIETLY, APPRECIATED.

ABOVE LEFT Once an Enigma key had been broken, ciphered messages were fed through Typex machines, to produce the clear German text. **ABOVE RIGHT** The staggering success of the whole operation – the sheer weight of messages intercepted, decrypted, translated and analysed – is illustrated by the fact that they ran out of shelf space for the fast-expanding cross-referencing card index files and had to line them up on the floor.

of some extraordinary espionage work, fought hard to keep pace. It wasn't always possible. The Germans had by now introduced the 'stecker board' to the Enigma; a further complication, involving wiring plugged in different ways according to each set-up of the machine. But by the summer of 1939, with the frightening noise of increasing German aggression carrying across the Polish border, there was a meeting in a forest near Pyry between the Polish mathematicians and Bletchley's senior cryptographer Dilly Knox, where they managed to pass on invaluable information about the way the machine was set up. Although Knox was apparently infuriated that the Poles had beaten him to the solution he had spent the last few years searching, Bletchley Park was given a terrific head start.

The Poles had also been working on methods of speeding up the checking of different combinations: there were the Zygalski sheets and the bomba machines. The sheet method was both ingenious and tortuously complex, very basically involving special sheets of perforated paper with grid square patterns of four squares of 26 by 26, and letters, all arranged on a light box, to calculate via painstaking mathematics possible Enigma wheel orders. The bombas (the term meaning 'ice cream') were not

wholly reliable machines, the idea of which was to run six sets of Enigma wheels simultaneously in order to search for repeated enciphered letters. They were considered less effective than the Zygalski sheets – but the basic idea of the bombas, the notion that machines could be made to do some of the heavy repetitive checking tasks, was taken up by Alan Turing and Gordon Welchman and refined into Bletchley's bombe machines. It was the crucial addition of an electrical 'diagonal board' – which in a symbolic sense rather mirrored the German innovation of the stecker board – that made this technical approach much more feasible. Cryptology was moving fast towards a wholly mechanised age. These bombe machines alone could not actually crack Enigma – but if fed 'cribs', or head starts, such as repetitive weather reports, or even friendly greetings between different German commanders, they could then power through thousands upon thousands of different combinations at a speed that no number of humans could get near. Enigma messages – from whatever part of the German war machine – were generated by dedicated operators working with code-books and pre-arranged settings that would change every 24 hours. The encrypted letters, illuminated on the lamp board, would be noted down by the Enigma operator,

RIGHT Alan Turing's revolutionary bombe machines clattered through thousands of code combinations at top speed with drums rotating ceaselessly.

BELOW They had to be tended night and day by Wrens, standing by to re-set them.

then transmitted by Morse code, the scrambled letters arranged into groups of four or five. It was those groupings that the codebreakers would then be examining after these messages were intercepted: column upon column of random letters in uniform groups. It's easy to see now just how daunting the prospect was. But the Poles, together with a French contingent and the British, saw another tiny sliver of light, another slender means of perhaps getting a firm foothold into the machine. One weak point in the Enigma encoding system – if such an esoteric aspect of the system might be termed 'weak' – was the fact that the machine would never encrypt a letter as itself. In other words, A would never become A. For anyone else, this aspect of its workings would be of little assistance. But the mathematicians and classicists combined were relentless in their attacks upon the entire structure of Enigma, and any means by which entry points might be forced.

The first two bombe machines – built by Harold 'Doc' Keen and the British Tabulating Company at Letchworth – made their Bletchley debut in the summer of 1940. Prior to this, Enigma had

been broken by hand, as it were, thanks to such leaps of insightful genius as the Herivel tip. Young mathematician John Herivel had, after the end of a long shift, returned home and set to imagining the German operators of Enigma. He imagined these straight-talking men, possibly using the names of their girlfriends in message preambles, or even jocular swear words. Herivel also imagined how they might set up the Enigma machines on each new day, and how they could be tempted to take shortcuts. Such shortcuts might be detected, and thus open up an entire trove of messages. The bombe machines could only be effective exactly because of this genius flash of psychological insight: once a shortcut or repetition was confirmed, the bombes could then set to work in earnest.

The bombes were large cabinets filled with rotating drums, and the back of each machine featured intricate wiring. Wrens worked throughout the night, keeping watch as the machines worked through their menus, and taking note whenever a bombe reached a 'stop' on the correct code-setting. It was often quite physically trying tending to the needs of these vast contraptions. The wiring had to be adjusted with tweezers and when there was a room full of the machines, some Wrens found the incessant noise quite difficult to deal with, though veteran Jean Valentine recalled for her own part that it wasn't actually all that bad – more like the 'clickety-ticking' of knitting, as she put it.

In 1940, the first two bombes had been conveyed to Bletchley under a shroud of utter secrecy (and in unostentatious lorries – the authorities did not want to excite curiosity by making a huge security song and dance of them). Soon thereafter, the numbers of these machines multiplied – some 210 bombes were built in all – and veteran Wrens now look at them with what might be described as mixed feelings. By the end of the War, in 1945, Harold Keen had received an OBE for his war work, for which he was warmly congratulated by his Hut 6 friend and collaborator Oliver

Lawn. After the end of the War, the machines at Bletchley Park were destroyed.

Another crucial – though oddly less celebrated – machine system in use at Bletchley Park was the Hollerith machine. This was an evolved version of a 19th-century innovation, invented by Herman Hollerith and used rather impressively to collate the 1890 US census. It was a punched-card system, much favoured by retail businesses such as department stores, that was adapted for Bletchley's purposes, first to act as an intelligence index, but also to help the codebreakers mechanically reduce the number of potential Enigma wheel settings that they would have to check. Unfortunately for the operators, whereas the bombe machines had at least a sort of hypnotic fascination about their clickety-ticking function, the Holleriths were a little more utilitarian. One veteran recalled being bored to tears as she learned how to punch information on to special cards, adding that the process became a little less tedious when it was automatic. The machines were used to look for 'four-letter repeats', in conjunction with platoons of linguists. There were various dizzying stages of information storage, running from the Collator, to the Reproducer, with intelligence

ABOVE At the Eastcote out-station, different bombes were allocated to separate territories.

RIGHT The top secret workshop in Letchworth where Harold 'Doc' Keene and Oliver Lawn oversaw the manufacture of the revolutionary bombe machines in 1940.

being saved on master cards. So even though it was some distance behind Alan Turing's revolutionary theories concerning machines that could be made to 'think', the Holleriths were still an early means of saving data mechanically.

Throughout those years, encryption technology was moving fast; several years into the War, the Germans were now also using a system termed Lorenz, known at Bletchley as 'Tunny' or 'Fish' because of its other German name, Sagefisch. These machines were described as 'non-Morse teleprinters' and worked with tape, using binary digits as the means of encoding messages. Lorenz was not a portable system and it was mainly intended for use by German High Command, to communicate directly with the headquarters of their field marshals. Whereas the Enigma messages – often sent from the field of battle – tended to be tactical, the Lorenz traffic was more about long-term strategy. To find a way into it would be a prize beyond value. Brigadier Tiltman was the first to do so, rather staggeringly by hand. Yet as with Enigma, the Germans kept on adding extra secure features to the apparatus and soon only a technological way into the code would be possible. Professor Max Newman and talented figures like W. (Bill) Tutte, and a department of the General Post Office situated in the London suburb of Dollis Hill, set to work. Their first answer to the Lorenz conundrum was a machine that they called – with

an element of self-deprecation, referring to his brilliantly comic drawings of mad inventions – the Heath Robinson.

In fact, this machine – a mass of wires and spools and paper tape – which made its debut in April/May 1943, was a brilliant stepping stone; using the new technique of photo-electronics, it was capable of reading 2,000 characters a second. It worked with closed loops of tape which were pulled through the machine via sprockets and pulleys. Unfortunately, it also had practical drawbacks, including a tendency for the paper tape to tear. Veterans recalled that, as a system, it was both maddeningly delicate to operate and fantastically frustrating when it quite frequently broke down. But it did prove that Professor Newman had hit the right principle; what was needed was a rather sturdier construction. In other words, this was not just a problem of codebreaking; this was an engineering challenge. In that Dollis

LEFT Dr Tommy Flowers of the GPO – a belatedly recognised engineering genius. There is now a road named after him in north-west London. After the War, he helped create the premium bond machine ERNIE.

FAR LEFT The later years of the War brought more complex Nazi codes – and still more complex technology to crack them in the form of the Colossus.

LEFT The Post Office Research station in Dollis Hill. In this quiet institute, on top of a hill overlooking London, Dr Tommy Flowers and his team experimented with new computer and innovative telephone technology.

TO BE KEPT UNDER LOCK AND KEY AND NEVER TO BE REMOVED FROM THE OFFICE
THIS FORM IS TO BE USED FOR AIR INTELLIGENCE MESSAGES ONLY

64 BLETCHLEY PARK: THE SECRET ARCHIVES

Hill GPO unit was a very talented man called Tommy Flowers; born in East Ham, educated at night school. Although there was some resistance from Gordon Welchman, who clearly did not quite trust this non-Oxbridge figure, Flowers combined his wits with Max Newman. The Flowers solution was a machine that would be called Colossus. Although not strictly a computer, it was the very clear antecedent. Before the War, Tommy Flowers had been working on telephone technology – he brought in electronic digital equipment that used huge numbers of vacuum tubes, an idea that he saw could be pressed into service elsewhere. The tapes of the Heath Robinson were now largely replaced by electronics: the first Colossus contained around 1,500 thermionic valves. It could read 5,000 characters a second. The later version had around 2,500 of these valves and could read even more quickly. Flowers realised that the most practical way to avoid this construction breaking down was very simply to never switch it off. There had been some objection to his procurement of so many valves; the furious memos in the archives now point to a period of great inter-departmental tension. But when Colossus started helping to crack messages from high-ranking German commanders to the office of Hitler himself, Flowers was triumphantly vindicated. In March 1944, almost as soon as it had started operation, Colossus managed to crowbar its way into correspondence between the Fuhrer and Gerd von Rundstedt, the Commander in Chief in the west. As we shall see in chapter nine, the impact of this upon D-Day was almost incalculable.

Visually, the Colossus was a beguiling, if complex creation. It was tall enough almost to touch the ceiling and wide enough to nearly fill the room. On one side, a bank of switches and tiny lights, flashing red and white; in the middle, further switches, a plug-board and, below this, a teleprinter that would chatter into life when the

correct setting for a code had been found. To look at the brilliant recreation at Bletchley Park now, you are irresistibly put in mind of old Quatermass films, or any number of quaint 1950s British science fiction epics. On the other side of this construction was the part that the operating Wrens must have dreaded most: multiple suspended reels, upon which ran the remaining paper-tape component. This would run at 30 miles per hour, and was infuriatingly prone to snapping and exquisitely hard to manoeuvre into position so that it would run smoothly at the start of every set-up.

It must also have taken some practise to learn how to operate with any confidence. Some Wrens recalled how there was almost a school-like induction for a couple of weeks beforehand: lessons involving desks and blackboards, and the principles of binary mathematics. But together with the difficulties, there was also a tremendous sense of pride among these young women. On any shift, it would tend to be one Wren looking after a Colossus machine while elsewhere in the room were codebreakers, usually mathematicians, foraging through the results. So while the work was hard, it was also absorbing. And even though the Wrens were not told the provenance of the information that their machines

were decoding, it was none the less obvious that it was vital. The War gave women opportunities in the workplace previously denied to them. The Newmanry and the Colossus was a step into one of the ultimate male-dominated inner sanctums: the world of technology.

What was little known at the time was that Tommy Flowers had been so determined that his ideas would work that he dipped into his own pocket in order to ensure that the machine was constructed. The effort, plus the financial sacrifice, paid off somewhat triumphantly. The first of these machines was such a success that eight others were ordered, as quickly as Flowers and his team could make them.

The reason the Colossus wasn't a computer was that it didn't have an internally stored program – each time it was set up, it had to be set up afresh. But these machines – soon there was an improved Mark II – were extremely fast and effective and the mere fact that this marvel of electronics worked at all is tribute to the engineering genius of Tommy Flowers. He demonstrated clearly that a computing age was within near reach; Professor Newman was inspired directly after the War to continue this line of research in Manchester.

OPPOSITE Built at the GPO Research Centre in London, the original Colossus was in some ways improvised, and parts of the appartus involved telephone exchange components.

LEFT Tending the Colossus: using revolutionary valve technology, this machine enabled the cryptologists to read the messages being sent out by German High Command. The machines required much more interaction from intensely trained Wren operators.

It is generally thought that after 1945, just two Colossus machines survived, transplanted to the new GCHQ base in Cheltenham. Then even these were destroyed. This was keenly felt by Dr Flowers, who had to consign his own files, notes and blueprints to a bonfire for security reasons – even if the original machines no longer existed, it was felt that even the design of them had to stay a strictly buried secret. Despite the fact that he had been awarded an MBE and £1,000 (a considerable sum back then), neither could make up for the aching sense of absence he felt as these machines – the most secret of all Bletchley's achievements – were reduced to their base components. Dr Flowers spent the rest of his career with the Post Office, and it was his belief that the complete cloak of secrecy around the Colossus actually held back any putative British computer industry just at the point that the Americans were starting to seize the initiative. Indeed, on the other side of the Atlantic, the Americans quite swiftly declassified the wartime research that they had done, leading to a boom in this new branch of computer science.

Recently, thanks to the late computer engineer Tony Sale, a dedicated team of volunteers at Bletchley Park have pulled off the quite extraordinary feat of constructing a replica working Colossus machine. It is a source of wonder to visitors – particularly the younger visitors – for it is in this machine that we see the true birth of the computer (despite competing claims from the US). It is easy to imagine this beast clattering and chattering in the concrete blocks throughout the silence of the night, the small lights winking white and red in mesmerising and seemingly random patterns, the tape spooling round in seemingly endless loops. It is also worth bearing in mind that in 1945, as the Park's activities were being wound down, Professor Newman told his young colleagues: 'We are losing the most interesting job that we ever had.'

FORTHCOMING
in this

The Wolverton Clu
DANGEROU
by J. B

on Saturday,

The Drama Grou

CHRISTI

Probable Dates :

Wednesc
30th

FULL CAST ON STAGE FOR FINALE
"COMBINED OPS"
(FIRST NIGHT).

6

Off-Duty Hours

ABOVE Glenn Miller and his band perform in an English meadow; the occasion of his July 1944 concert in Bedford caused huge excitement among Bletchley Wrens – American swing was quite the thing.

B.P. DRAMA GROUP

presents

Pride and Prejudice

A Sentimental Comedy in Three Acts
by Helen Jerome
adapted from the Novel by Jane Austen

Tuesday, 4th May
to
Saturday, 8th May, 1943

THERE ARE SOME BLETCHLEY VETERANS WHO GET A LITTLE ANNOYED WHEN ANY MENTION IS MADE OF THEIR OFF-DUTY HOURS. THEY WERE THERE TO PLAY THEIR PART IN DEFEATING HITLER, AFTER ALL; NOT TO PUT ON CABARETS. CAPTAIN JERRY ROBERTS, MBE, REMEMBÉRS THAT EVEN IF HE HAD WANTED TO JOIN ANY OF THE MULTIPLICITY OF SOCIETIES THAT BLETCHLEY PARK HAD TO OFFER, HE WAS SIMPLY BILLETED TOO FAR AWAY, AND THERE WAS TOO LITTLE TIME.

Others, though, remembered that Bletchley Park had an extraordinarily rich cultural life. Of course, yes, the work was hard. And that is the point: it was so intense and so exhausting that the codebreakers and everyone else needed some inventive and involving ways to unwind. Given that some of the finest minds of a generation were gathered here, it is perhaps not surprising that their leisure hours were more highbrow than those of others.

Even from the earliest years, for instance, there were Christmas and midsummer revues – composed of comic sketches and songs – which were staged rather elaborately, with costumes and sets. The younger codebreakers would write amusing songs to do with their working conditions and the insanity of life at the Park. The sketches were more broadly satirical, aimed at enemies and Allies alike. In 1945, the revue was called 'It's The End, Let's Face It', and featured jokes to do with Ibsen and Purcell. In a revue a few years previously, senior codebreaker Josh Cooper had taken part, dressed up in desert fatigues because, as his son later pointed out, he had been in Palestine in the 1920s and had the 'costume' handy. The audiences were always

PYGMALION

BY
GEORGE BERNARD SHAW

CAST

ELIZA DOOLITTLE	Sgt. Jeanne Cammaerts
PROFESSOR HENRY HIGGINS	Sgt. Derek Davies
COLONEL PICKERING	L/Cpl. David Alun Pugh
ALFRED DOOLITTLE (Eliza's father)	L/Cpl. Eddie Underwood
MRS. HIGGINS (Higgins' mother)	Sgt. Betty Hickman
MRS. PEARCE (Higgins' housekeeper)	Sgt. Iris Gargery
MRS. EYNSFORD HILL	L/Cpl. Penelope Alexander
MISS EYNSFORD HILL	L/Cpl. Pamela Clayton
FREDDY EYNSFORD HILL	Cpl. John Thompson
PARLOURMAID	Cpl. Norah Mantell
A SARCASTIC BYSTANDER	Pte. Douglas Keyte
ANOTHER BYSTANDER	Cpl. Michael Pocock

The Play produced by Cpl. Tom Gauge.

ACT. 1. Covent Garden. Late evening.
ACT. 2. Professor Higgins' Laboratory.
The next morning.
ACT. 3. Mrs. Higgins' Drawing Room.
Three months later.
ACT. 4. Professor Higgins' Laboratory.
Three months later.
ACT. 5. Mrs. Higgins' Drawing Room.
The next morning.

President	Capt. N. Somers
Stage Manager	Sgt. Richard Pendlebury
Production Secretary	Sgt. Jessie Sillence
Lighting	Leslie Edwards
Scene Painting	L/Cpl. Cecil Waller
Business Manager	Major F. S. Andrews

Stage Staff Sgt. Maurice Lynch, Cpl. Henry Balen, L/Cpl. Walter Grundy, L/Cpl. Peter Sweeting, Sgt. Hugh Dent, L/Cpl. John Simms.

There will be one interval of three minutes and three of ten minutes.

The Committee wish to express their grateful acknowledgement to the B.P. Drama Group, B.P. Dance Committee, and the Bletchley Co-operative Society for help and advice.

The next production will be

TWELFTH NIGHT
January 16th, 17th, 1945.

Printer, Bletchley.

enthusiastic. As a teenager, messenger Mimi Galilee attended these shows and looked on with wonder at these 'amazing beings'. It is not difficult to detect potential influences; drawn from Oxford and particularly Cambridge, had the war not broken out these clever young men (and they were mostly the men) might very well have auditioned for Footlights, or similar revue societies. The Bletchley revues also had the effect of making operatives laugh affectionately and fondly at the institution in which they worked.

There were those who wanted something a little more nutritious from a night out at the theatre, and Bletchley's actors – some of whom were indeed actually actors in the outside world – staged commendably inventive productions of Much Ado About Nothing, Gaslight, They Came to a City and French Without Tears, among others.

For the carefully-built sets, and the elaborate costumes, they often had help with materials from sources such as the Bletchley Co-Operative Society. Sometimes, unlikely stars were born; Ann

THIS PAGE AND OPPOSITE
It wasn't all Shakespeare, Austen and JB Priestley: the codebreakers also had a gift for comedy and music. Amusingly prominent in many programme notes is Brin Newton-John – codebreaker and father of singer Olivia.

BALLET SCENE ROSEMARY CARVILL

FULL CAST ON STAGE FOR FINALE "COMBINED OPS" (FIRST NIGHT).

Dent recalled Jeanne Cammaerts, 'a big and imposing girl' who showed 'considerable talent' as Eliza Doolittle in a production of Pygmalion that featured a colleague from the Sergeants' Mess as Professor Higgins.

Another point about these productions, which were taken out to halls and auditoriums around the county, was that they raised money for various military benevolent funds. The audiences who came from villages and towns thereabouts would have had no idea what these young people on stage were doing in the way of war work; but judging by local newspapers from 1945, after the war ended, one of the regrets was that the area was losing such a fascinating theatrical troupe. 'We don't know what they did at the Park,' wrote the correspondent, 'but their productions were much admired.' Some of Bletchley's proper professional actors – notably Dorothy Hyson – maintained a little of that limelight glamour even during their daytime duties in the huts. Hyson, a great West End theatrical name, not to mention an erstwhile co-star to the phenomenally popular George Formby – was noted particularly for her white chinchilla coats, which made many other women almost literally groan with envy. At that stage, Hyson, who was married, was conducting an affair with her future husband, the Special Operations Executive (SOE) agent (and fellow actor) Anthony Quayle, who on rare occasions would come to visit her in Bletchley.

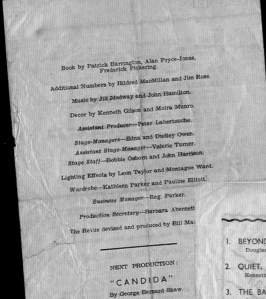

Book by Patrick Barrington, Alan Pryce-Jones, Frederick Pickering.

Additional Numbers by Hildred MacMillan and Jim Rose.

Music by Jill Medway and John Hamilton.

Decor by Kenneth Gilson and Moira Munro.

Assistant Producer—Peter Labertouche.

Stage-Managers—Edna and Dudley Owen.

Assistant Stage-Manager—Valerie Turner.

Stage Staff—Bobbie Osborn and John Harrison.

Lighting Effects by Leon Taylor and Montague Ward.

Wardrobe—Kathleen Parker and Pauline Elliott.

Business Manager—Reg. Parker.

Production Secretary—Barbara Aberneth

The Revue devised and produced by Bill Ma

NEXT PRODUCTION :

"CANDIDA"

By George Bernard Shaw

February 21st to 25th

Produced by Pamela Gibson.

B.P. DRAMA GROUP

presents

Pride and Prejudice

A Sentimental Comedy in Three Acts

by Helen Jerome

adapted from the Novel by Jane Austen

Tuesday, 4th May
to
Saturday, 8th May, 1943

P·R·O·G·R·A·M·M·E

1. BEYOND THE PALE
   Douglas Jones and most of the Company.

2. QUIET, PLEASE !
   Kenneth Gilson.

3. THE BABY NAVY
   Paul Stephenson, Frederick Pickering, Malcolm Howgate, Reg Parker, Richard Bright.

4. BRING ME MY BEAU
   Bill Marchant, Vera Naismith, Kenneth Gilson.

5. NO BLOSSOMS FOR MR. BANQUO
   Olivia Morrell, June Canney, Shella Dunlop, Douglas Jones, David Warwick, Mary Tate, Brin Newton-John, Paul Stephenson, Patrick Barrington.

6. CUPBOARD LOVE
   Peggy Appleton, Elizabeth Langstaff, Reg Parker, Peter Labertouche.

7. LULLABY
   Esther Jones, Barbara Brown, Mary Tate, Brin Newton-John.

8. AT SMOKEY JOE'S
   Olivia Morrell, Peggy Appleton, June Canney, Shella Dunlop, Peter Labertouche, Richard Bright, Reg. Parker, Malcolm Howgate, Kenneth Gilson, Frederick Pickering, Shaun Wylie, David Warwick.

9. COLOUR BAR
   Douglas Jones.

10. MURDER IN THE CAFETERIA
    Pamela Gibson, Olivia Morrell, Shirley Rhodes, Paul Stephenson, Shaun Wylie, Patrick Barrington.

THANK YOU, KIND SIR
June Canney, Brin Newton-John.

12. LIGHT ENSATAINMENT
    Bill Marchant, Mary Tate, Diana Marchant, Vera Naismith, Douglas Jones, Frederick Pickering, Jill Medway.

INTERVAL

13. LEBENSRAUM
    June Canney, Shella Dunlop, Vera Naismith, Diana Marchant, Olivia Morrell, Shirley Rhodes, Esther Jones.

14. RAT-A-PLAN, RAT-A-PLAN
    Brin Newton-John, Richard Bright, Paul Stephenson, Elizabeth Langstaff, Malcolm Howgate, Kenneth Gilson, Shaun Wylie, Pamela Gibson, Bill Marchant.

15. WARNING TO WANTONS
    Douglas Jones.

16. L'APRES-MIDI D'UN PHONE
    Brin Newton-John, Peggy Appleton.

17. EVANGELINE—OR NO GOOD DEED GOES UNPUNISHED
    Malcolm Howgate, Reg Parker, Pamela Gibson, Elizabeth Langstaff, Shaun Wylie, Kenneth Gilson, Peter Labertouche, Frederick Pickering.

18. SHADRACK
    Paul Stephenson, Vera Naismith, Diana Marchant, David Warwick.

19. IT'S A FOUL WIND THAT BLOWS OUT OF A FOOTBALL
    Kenneth Gilson.

20. SOUFFLET SENTIMENTAL
    Bill Marchant, Esther Jones, Mary Tate, Barbara Brown, Brin Newton-John, Kenneth Gilson, Diana Marchant, Vera Naismith, Shella Dunlop, Douglas Jones.

21. SWINE SONG
    Frederick Pickering.

22. BUT ONCE A YEAR
    The Company.

At the Pianos—Jill Medway and John Hamilton.

The Park's greatest theatrical talent happened to be one of its most experienced codebreakers, with World War One cryptology successes under his belt. Frank Birch, who as mentioned elsewhere had essayed a successful Widow Twankey, had, earlier in his career, been a history don at Cambridge. He had given that up in 1928 to be a theatrical producer and director, and had staged warmly reviewed productions at the Cambridge Festival Theatre. One of his young company then was Jessica Tandy, later to find Hollywood fame. He also produced an English version of Goldoni's comedy, The Servant of Two Masters, in 1932. This was rather less rapturously received than its 21st-century smash-hit incarnation, better known as One Man, Two Guvnors.

After the War, Birch became better known as a regular BBC broadcaster, and was a contributor to the popular radio show, The Brains Trust. Oddly, at Bletchley, Birch was actually known less for theatricals than for his unyielding style of man management. He was one of the few in the hierarchy who seriously attempted to impose proper discipline on the intellects working for him, and was occasionally resented for it.

One of the curiosities of Bletchley Park was that it was filled not just with mathematicians, but talented musicians too. The two

ABOVE LEFT The house itself was a focus for socialising; while the ballroom echoed to the sound of waltzes, the front lawn was sometimes used for the surreal spectacle of Highland dancing displays or simply tea breaks.

ABOVE RIGHT Cycling was hugely popular; many women had second-hand bikes and relished the chance – and the freedom – to take off into the country.

OPPOSITE TOP After long shifts behind blackouts, it was genuinely important for codebreakers to soak up as much sun – and vitamin D – as they could in leisure hours. One hut had a solarium for gloomier weather.

sometimes crossed over, but this also meant that codebreakers and Wrens had a feast of musical opportunities. The Park authorities managed to secure visits from famous artistes such as the tenor Peter Pears (lover of Benjamin Britten) and the pianist Myra Hess. In part, this was due to Sergeant Herbert Murrill who, as mentioned in Chapter Four, was the BBC's director of music,

Younger Bletchley-ites were finding that their musical tastes had more of an American swing. There was terrific excitement among the Wrens later in the War when Glenn Miller and his band played in nearby Bedford. This was largely for the benefit of US troops – but many young British women who went along to these shows, with their heady atmospheres, recalled them swooningly.

The codebreakers and the Wrens needed a great deal of physical exercise too. Since the work either involved being hunched over bigram tables or wrestling with the vast bombe machines, often late into the night, both fresh air and sunshine were clearly important. Many of the Bletchley recruits got hold of bicycles, and would take themselves off into the countryside on precious days off. Sometimes they would venture further, and take rowing boats down rivers. Oliver Lawn and Sheila MacKenzie did this while they were courting, taking a picnic with them. Unfortunately, they got caught in a monstrous deluge while in the middle of the river and far from cover. But not even that could spoil their day. Within the grounds of Bletchley Park itself, exercise was

and therefore fantastically well connected. Piano chords could be heard all over the Park; many of the young codebreakers in the Huts were rather fine performers on the instrument. It was also the case – certainly in middle-class families – that youngsters would have been much more familiar with such instruments in the home than most of their age would be now.

But it wasn't all just Brahms, or the codebreakers' madrigal society singing on the banks of the Grand Union Canal in the warm rosy sunset of a summer's evening.

not neglected. Since the days of the former owners, the Leons, the estate boasted tennis courts, and the Bletchley Tennis Society was very popular. In the archives is a fascinating letter from the secretary to the Dunlop company, pleading (in those straitened, rationed times) for a new supply of balls. There is also a beseeching internal memo, asking that the members of the tennis club be allowed to use the Summer House as a changing

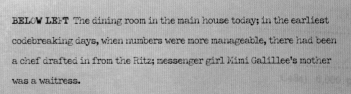

ABOVE LEFT The new Bletchley Park museum canteen offers a wider range of delicacies than Woolton Pie (featuring volumes of potatoes and turnips) and salad leaves with stray insects – all of which were wolfed by the codebreakers.

BELOW LEFT The dining room in the main house today; in the earliest codebreaking days, when numbers were more manageable, there had been a chef drafted in from the Ritz; messenger girl Mimi Galillee's mother was a waitress.

Dear Commander Travis

I hope you will forgive my for bothering you with
the matter to be outlined below, but I am confident that you will help me. I write this on behalf
of the younger element at B.P., who are anxious to
conserve their physical fitness despite the shortage of daylight hours and the somewhat sedentary
life. Last year we organized a hockey club, the
members of which were very enthusiastic until they
saw and experienced the type of ploughed field
that that had to be played on for want of something better, their enthusiasm waning until the
whole thing had to be given up. Determined that
the same fate should not meet our efforts this
year I felt encouraged by the success of the military section which obtained the loan of the school
ground just below the park, we approached the
headmaster of the school to see if he could also
allow the civil servants to use the ground for
about one hour in the week.

We were told that the ground was being used extensively already and that it would be over-using it
to allow anyone else on.

I would suggest that this is a rather exaggerated
assessment of the situation, and that the pretext
was made use of in order to get rid of us, as it
were. Would you be good enough to make an official
or semi-official demand for the use of the
field?....

LEFT Physical fitness
was a constant concern,
as this memo concerning
a Bletchley hockey team
illustrates. Alan Turing
went on prodigious long-
distance runs, and could
finish a marathon in two
hours and forty minutes.

THIS PAGE In deepest winter, when the lake froze over, there was a craze for skating which became seriously competitive; the Americans always seemed to have the better skates. Note the rather spirited accordion accompaniment. There was always some form of music in the air at Bletchley

room. Given the security around all areas of the Park, and the fact that there were rooms and buildings that it was forbidden for anyone to enter, the request is not so frivolous as it sounds.

In the earliest days, games of rounders had been played just in front of the house, with the teams stacked with dons and classicists, as witnessed by an incredulous Malcolm Muggeridge. On sunny days, the lake just a few yards down from the house was popular with the Wrens. They would row out into the middle of the water, come under attack from the perpetually furious geese, and then row back. That same lake froze over several times throughout the winters of the war, and when it did so, the codebreakers took to it with an almost childlike gusto. The American codebreakers were particularly envied for their skating skills. On warmer spring days, many Wrens remembered how they would sometimes simply flop by the water with a cup of coffee after a gruelling eight-hour shift, soaking up the welcome sun after work conducted in blackout conditions.

On top of all this, there was perhaps the greatest obsession of all, and that was with dancing. Elsewhere, we have seen how

ABOVE Distinguished visitors to the Park occasionally glimpsed the wonderful spectacle of Oxbridge dons playing rounders in the grounds.

LEFT The Bletchley fencing society was a great hit; members managed to find a local tutor. Gentler pursuits included rambling and bird-watching. All these were crucial to help codebreakers shake off stress.

Hugh Foss was the undisputed master of the Gay Gordons; but the Bletchley operatives were much more varied in their moves than that. One veteran recalled the noise like thunder as ballroom dancing classes were held in the main house's ballroom and kitchen. Then there were the dances held at American bases across the county, for which there was a particular clamour among the Wrens to get to. One veteran Wren recalled the fun of those evenings, and the strategy that she employed to bat off any questions about her secret work: she told inquisitive American soldiers that it was her job 'to scrape the barnacles off the bottoms of submarines'. Apparently no one questioned this any further. The Wren added that while the Americans were certainly generous with nylons and cigarettes, as per the old cliché, the cigarettes were Camels, they tasted horrible, and the tobacco kept falling out of them.

Wrens would be taken to these dances on buses; there were also occasions at Woburn when the men – be they RAF or codebreakers – were sent by bus for the evening dances at the village hall. This wasn't just a Bletchley phenomenon, of course – there were many young women who practically lived for their dances throughout the War. But the Wrens went at it with unusual energy. The Bletchley Y out-station in Scarborough, Yorkshire, became so noted among Morse-listening Wrens that many women in other stations applied to be transferred there because they had heard it was such fun. Added to this, back in Bletchley and the villages around, there were wildly popular village hops, though veteran Jean Valentine says that as an 18-year-old who had led a sheltered life up until that point, she never forgot her shock

TO BE KEPT UNDER LOCK AND KEY AND NEVER TO BE REMOVED FROM THE OFFICE. THIS FORM IS TO BE USED FOR AIR INTELLIGENCE MESSAGES ONLY

78 BLETCHLEY PARK: THE SECRET ARCHIVES

at one such occasion when a local young mother started breast-feeding her baby. More than all this, though, the dances were where countless romances were sealed.

The Park had more cerebral pursuits too, including a book club, language courses, and an early film club. You could, if you wished, sign up to learn Latin or Russian. There was a classical music appreciation society, though its limited repertoire of records got rather worn out on the Park's gramophone; late on in the War, an official request was put in for the purchase of quite an expensive 'radiogram'.

Given the backgrounds of so many codebreakers, naturally there were chess clubs too; one Wren remembered being on the train with British champion Hugh Alexander when he had a couple of days' leave. He was sitting there with a practice set because later that day he would be taking on all-comers in a super-chess tournament in Cambridge.

The point of all these pursuits went far beyond mere leisure; the staff of Bletchley Park were being invited to de-pressurise after gruelling six-day weeks and all-night shifts with pursuits that – while entertaining and diverting – would keep their minds and bodies occupied. It was about physical well-being, but their mental health too. When you have been working under unfathomable pressure, knowing that the job you are doing is vital for saving so many lives, how would it even be possible to sleep properly unless you and your colleagues could find ways to focus fully on something else, like Shakespeare or a comic revue?

BELOW At the end of the War, local Buckinghamshire newspapers regretted that the Bletchley players would be seen no more. The critics never had any idea of the work they did, but they admired their productions.

"SHOULDER OF MUTTON," FAR BLETCHLEY

7

Bletchley the Wartime Town

LEFT Unlike today's rather drab concrete 1970s rebuild, Bletchley railway station was once a large and lively junction. Wartime recruits would either be picked up by car, or simply walk from there along the side of the adjoining Bletchley Park estate.

A TUCK CARD

ABOVE Even throughout the War, hunting remained an integral part of country life near Bletchley; RSS analyst Hugh Trevor-Roper made excuses to visit Bletchley Park so that he could actually ride out with the Whaddon Hunt.

OPPOSITE The area's small sweet shops – and the severe rationing – were recalled by veteran Mimi Galillee, who was a teenage messenger with a very sweet tooth.

For some recruits, arrival at Bletchley station in the thick darkness of the blackout was a suspenseful matter: with no lights to guide them, their footsteps would echo on the iron bridge and then they would be met at the station's booking office by someone who would take them the short distance into the nation's most intensely secret institution. For others, the first sight of Bletchley was rather more quotidian. One codebreaker recalled how, one afternoon as he got off that train for the first time, he was greeted on the platform by a cheeky young 'urchin', who shouted, ''ere, mister, I'll read your secret writing for ya!' before running off.

It was never the most inspirational of towns. 'I spent a month in Bletchley — last Sunday,' was one Naval Intelligence wisecrack that did the rounds. Particularly for those who had been recruited from London, there was something of a culture shock. One young woman linguist recalled curtly that the place was 'a dump'. Bletchley at that time had two industries: the railways and brickworks. The landscape around had been carved out for these works. And the manufactories produced a distinctive smell that would catch the back of the throat on warm summer's days.

Into this broadly working-class milieu were thrown hundreds and thousands of mostly middle-class recruits. It is difficult to know who would have found the adjustment harder to make. One young lady spirited down from well-to-do Edinburgh found herself in an outlying satellite village, Wolverton, billeted with a couple who were polite enough but who would inevitably tell her the day after an exhausting night shift, 'We heard you come in', as though the young woman had any control over her hours. Another young woman, who was Catholic, was billeted with a family who were Plymouth Brethren, and who would not even allow

a radio to be played on the grounds that it was the devil's work. One Easter, the young woman begged to be able to listen to a performance of The Messiah. She was allowed, but throughout it all the father sang his own choice of hymns.

Yet we must also see it from the point of view of the billetors taking in these exotic creatures. The novelist-to-be Angus Wilson, whose Pompeiian mood swings were a source of wonder at the Park, dwelt with a kind family in a small house in the village of

Simpson. His prodigious consumption of cigarettes caused them, in vain, to make theatrical coughing noises to deter him. But the discomfort worked both ways. The only book anyone in the family ever appeared to read (and re-read) was Bunyan's Holy War; this must have seemed suffocating to the young writer and it has been suggested that it may have contributed to his ever-deepening depression. In a time when most young men were in uniform, Wilson's carefully chosen attire – rich blue shirts with apricot-coloured bow ties were a favoured combination – were a local talking point. But the claustrophobia of the billet, of the Park and of the little village bordered by the Victorian canal became too much for him. There was said to have been an incident where he threw an inkpot at a Wren. 'Angus isn't really mad,' said one of his colleagues later. 'He threw inkpots at all the right people.' In a wider sense, many in these small towns and villages could not help but disapprove of all these seemingly peculiar young men who did not appear to have proper wartime roles and who were not, as far as anyone could tell, pulling their weight. One local explanation for Bletchley Park was that it was a special lunatic asylum. Recruits such as Wilson would have done nothing to dispel this misconception.

TOP Codebreakers note that billeting in Bletchley was sometimes spartan but generally friendly. Codebreaker Keith Batey was moved by his widowed landlady's generosity with rations.

ABOVE Bletchley had cafes and fish and chip shops; the British Restaurant was largely shunned except by a few Scottish codebreakers, who liked the plain fare.

LEFT The town was so determinedly austere that the directorate was initially concerned that smarter recruits from London – used to neon lights and ritzy night-clubs – would sink into depression.

"SHOULDER OF MUTTON." FAR BLETCHLEY   A TUCK CARD

ABOVE Codebreakers such as Hugh Alexander and Stuart Milner-Barry adored the Shoulder of Mutton – the good cheer and the beer were the ideal antidote to the strains of their work. There was a local rumour that codebreakers would converse in Ancient Greek over their pints.

BELOW AND RIGHT Bletchley had a good range of shops, from fishmongers to jewellers. One local hairdresser salon got security clearance to visit the Park twice a week to offer the ladies shampoos and sets.

On top of this, as mentioned, a great many debutantes were recruited to work at Bletchley Park; some of them had been brought up in stately homes. The contrast for them was stark. One recalled the murderous cold of a house with an unheated parlour. Another lodged with a couple – the father worked in one of the brickworks – and their very boisterous children. One young woman – of distinct Bloomsbury leanings – sought to combat the intense pressure of the Bletchley work by retiring to her modest billet in off-duty hours and sitting in bed drinking quantities of gin and orange. A smart card-index girl was posted to a house that, to her relief, had the luxury of a bathroom. However, it did not have the luxury of a lock on the door. The woman of the house told the girl not to worry – she could take baths while the man of the house was out

working nights on the railways. That first night, the girl did just that, with some trepidation; just as she relaxed, undressed and got into the bath, the man of the house walked straight in, having managed to bunk off his shift. The girl made arrangements to move to a new billet shortly afterwards.

Like most small towns in the War, Bletchley could at least boast two cinemas (codebreakers loved to lose themselves in escapist

ABOVE RIGHT There was a discreet military presence at Bletchley Park and in the town. But at the Park itself, there was never a sense of military hierarchy. Men in uniform would sometimes to be told not to be so rigid about it.

BELOW Some codebreakers were – to their great irritation – pulled into the Home Guard. They were annoyed by having to 'run around at night with cork-blackened faces'.

dramas such as The Song of Bernadette and outlandish horrors like The Ghost of Frankenstein). There was also a British Restaurant (a chain started with the aim of promoting healthy rationing options, but which was remembered by veterans as being many rungs below the local fish and chip shop, the grub in the local pubs, and indeed Bletchley's very own canteen, which had little enough to shout about itself).

THE BEDFORD OUTPOST

BACK IN THE 1930S, WHEN THE STORM WAS GATHERING, EXPERT CRYPTANALYST JOHN TILTMAN, HAVING MASTERED SO MANY SOVIET CIPHERS, SMARTLY TURNED HIS LASER FOCUS ON TO JAPANESE CODES. WHEN WAR WITH JAPAN WAS AT LAST DECLARED IN DECEMBER 1941, HE WAS ACUTELY AWARE OF A SHORTAGE OF JAPANESE LINGUISTS. AND SO IT WAS THAT ABOVE A GAS SHOWROOM IN THE TOWN OF BEDFORD, SOME 15 MILES FROM BLETCHLEY PARK, BRIGADIER TILTMAN, WITH CAPTAIN OSWALD TUCK, SET ABOUT GIVING CLASSES TO CAREFULLY SELECTED YOUNG CLASSICS UNDERGRADUATES (MANY OF WHOM LATER WENT ON TO BE EMINENT ACADEMICS). CLASSICISTS WERE FELT TO HAVE MORE LINGUISTIC FLEXIBILITY THAN MATHEMATICIANS. TILTMAN WOULD NOT ENROL ANYONE WHO HAD ATTENDED CHARTERHOUSE SCHOOL; HIS CURIOUS PREJUDICE WAS THAT PRODUCTS OF THAT SCHOOL NEVER REALLY GREW UP. THE AMERICANS NATURALLY WERE WORKING ON THE SAME JAPANESE ENCRYPTION PROBLEMS; AND TODAY, IN US CIPHER CIRCLES, THE NAME OF BRIGADIER TILTMAN IS STILL MUCH REVERED.

The high street had the staples: a fishmonger, grocer, pharmacy, two butchers. It also had a hairdressing salon and, on top of this, a small department store. Women, with their clothing ration coupons, generally seemed to find the latter a shade too expensive, and would prefer, when they could, to get the train south into Watford to replenish their wardrobes. Bletchley also had a multitude of pubs; popular among the male codebreakers was the Shoulder of Mutton. As well as the pints and the darts, the landlady there was a gifted cook. At that time, women did not generally frequent pubs and locals were surprised when senior codebreaker Dilly Knox took his young prodigy Mavis Lever to a saloon bar for a gin and tonic. It was obvious by the expression on her face after the first sip that she was not an experienced drinker.

The church did not seem to figure quite as largely in the life of Bletchley as perhaps it did in smaller communities. But there was a thriving Methodist congregation, which was joined by codebreakers Oliver Lawn and Sheila MacKenzie (depending on their work rotas). One local vicar of an outlying village was unwittingly the cause of one of Bletchley's rare security scares. He had several young codebreakers billeted with him and made it his mission to discover exactly what it was they were doing up at the Park. Naturally, they were forbidden to tell him and his questioning grew both more forceful and more devious, until it reached a point that he was reported. A memo in the archives from the Bletchley directorate recommended the clergyman be given a 'thorough frightening': 'he is not a bad man, but he is a foolish one'.

But if the billets – with their lack of bathrooms, and indeed lack of indoor lavatories – were to some an unexpected trial, the countryside that lay all around came as a pleasant surprise. Those with bicycles would relish the chance to shake off the oppressive pressure of work by taking off on quiet roads to

explore. A few of the codebreakers were keen ramblers – this was a time when access to private land was a fiercely fought and rather radical cause – and the landscape was felt to be particularly rewarding for distance walkers. These ramblers also had other enthusiasms, such as for butterflies, and bird-watching. Again, in a time before vast soulless prairie farming, the small fields and gentle hills of Buckinghamshire were a treasure trove. Even the immediate scarred vicinity of the town, with the vast holes carved out of the earth for the brickworks, proved full of interesting wildlife.

But what of the town itself? An early Bletchley Park internal memo spoke of the Directorate's anxiety that Bletchley would prove too much of a culture shock for sophisticated young undergraduates swarming in from London, Oxford and Cambridge; that it would have a deadening effect that might sap morale. What they had not counted on was the infinite adaptability of the young, nor indeed the more reflective pleasures to be found in

an unassuming town, and indeed the way that it was possible to make their own entertainment. Bletchley's straightforwardness was clearly, to many, a refreshing contrast to the byzantine complexities and the frequently nocturnal pressure of life within the Park itself.

For local aristocrats and landowners, pleasure came in the form of the Whaddon Hunt – and indeed, the hunt was frequently joined by senior Radio Security Service man Hugh Trevor-Roper, who was in regular liaison with the Park. The hunt would tear across the Buckinghamshire countryside; on one occasion, the unhappy fox fled straight through military police security and into the grounds of Bletchley Park itself. This was obviously off-limits to the riders; all save one. Trevor-Roper, it has been suggested, had his security pass with him, and was able for a time at least to chase the fox in the hope that it would shoot back out of the gates again.

When some of the veterans returned to the rescued Park in the 1990s, for the first time since 1945, they found that while the

to go swimming in the pools left by the clay pits.

BELOW Even up until the 1960s – before nearby Milton Keynes blossomed outwards in all its futurism – the town of Bletchley remained remarkably un-notable. Architectual chronicler Nikolaus Pevsner couldn't recommend a single feature to his readers.

NAME			
FILE No.	V/HN/353		
Dial Read'g	KC/S	R.S.T.	CALL AS SENT
	5400	438	CZE de
	5400	438	GGG
	5200		
	4880		WER de RK

8

The Worldwide Listeners

LEFT Colombo, Sri Lanka. Hundreds of Wrens were sent out here to monitor Japanese codes. A great many of them – who had never before left Britain – were utterly bewitched by the life they found there.

Month	Year	GROUP OR G.S. BAND	CENTRE	Sheet No.
12	41		kc/s to	

SIGNALS HEARD, ETC

N.B. (i) ENTER PREAMBLE AND FIRST GROUP OF TEXT. (ii) WHEN ON A.W. (iii) ALL OBSERVATIONS OR NOTES TO BE IN BRACKETS.

* CONTROL * ANSWER

SAØ PSE CALL = K = SRI QSAØ QRX
W ¥3 GB SK WAT
= IIK ND 22ND 34 QRM (QRM BLOTTED
C (LISTENED TILL 1815 BUT ND) ST
C ET 935/71 = (VY HEAVY ATMOSPHERIC

OHLC	VUBAK	-NKUZ	MHPXN
FGEL	WOFYH	RDZFZ	RZAXP
YHNW	OPLDU	NECIW	FSJGS
VDQX	WBDMJ	MHRWW	NKLFW
HZGQ	OOVKW	CZEHQ	MWEKE
ZQDD	MIWF	VXAOU	KOVVW

T W35 PSE QSY (Parts of this may be o th
T T---FX Stations. I could hear o

K IIH	APSY-	OYIIR	LCHUP
JHHO	RIPBG	WLYRY	MMTUR
FDQY	EOVEG	PQEZB	IUVCU

N.B. WHEN NOT APPLICABLE AND IGNORE CENTRAL DIVISION.

I N A DIGITAL AGE, WHERE EVERY LAST BREATH AND THE ELECTRONIC PULSE CAN BE INSTANTLY RECORDED AND ANALYSED, IT IS INSTRUCTIVE TO THINK BACK JUST 75 YEARS, TO AN AGE WHEN THE WEB OF INTELLIGENCE AND ITS COMPLEX WORLDWIDE THREADS RELIED ALMOST WHOLLY ON THE QUICK-WITTEDNESS, INTENSE CONCENTRATION AND NIMBLE FINGERS OF SHARP YOUNG MINDS. MORSE CODE IS NOW A DYING ART, A LANGUAGE AS ESOTERIC AS ANCIENT GREEK. BUT TO THOUSANDS OF YOUNG RECRUITS IN THE WAR, SIGNED UP AND SWORN TO SECRECY TO PLAY THEIR ROLES IN THE BLETCHLEY CODEBREAKING OPERATION, IT BECAME SECOND NATURE. EVEN NOW, THERE ARE SOME VETERANS WHO HEAR A SNATCH OF MORSE CODE IN A FILM AND CAN INSTANTLY TRANSLATE IT.

An operation as vast as Bletchley Park required a dizzying supply of raw material, most of which was encoded messages, sent by German Enigma operators and plucked from the airwaves by dedicated secret listeners. For this work – in Britain and in stations right the way across the world – many thousands of Wrens and male wireless operators were deployed. That lightning ability to translate Morse was the most basic of the qualifications these young people needed. They required prodigious energy and patience; also a certain mental flexibility. Without it, they would have swiftly burned out. More than this: as the war went on, an unprecedented number of young women were despatched to the remoter regions of the earth, to carry out their vital work closer to the front line than any women had been before. Recruits to the 'Y' Service – the 'Y' was simply a phonetic abbreviation for 'wireless' – were brave pioneers in many ways.

Some years even before the advent of Enigma encoding technology, the science of radio – and the military impact that it could have – had preoccupied all the major powers since the inception of the medium. The ability to transmit messages without

the need for wires or cables could add terrific speed and stealth to any military manoeuvre. And it was also vital to be able to hear and interpret the conversations of your enemies. Wireless interception became a staple element in futuristic British thriller novels of the late Edwardian era. In real life, the number of small clandestine stations dedicated to listening to foreign signals – from the base on south London's Denmark Hill, which intercepted coded traffic from foreign embassies, to larger coastal operations such as the establishment in Scarborough, Yorkshire – were already very focused by the inter-war years. Thanks in large part to

OPPOSITE (above) The pristine white Wren uniforms for the Tropics. On parade in Colombo, Sri Lanka. Nightlife involved sophisticated restaurants and dances. (below) Less exotic (but still greatly enjoyed by many Wrens) – a posting to the Isle of Man, where much of the secret interception training work was done.

Brigadier Gambier-Parry – a radio enthusiast who had been one of the very first press officers for the fledgling BBC in the 1920s – military intelligence was embracing the fast-developing technology. And unlike some other elements in the British military at that time, it was very well prepared when war finally came.

It helped immeasurably, of course, that Britain still had an empire. From Hong Kong(China) to Ceylon (now Sri Lanka), from Bombay to the colour and heat of Egypt, there were not just highly trained operatives chasing ever elusive enemy frequencies; there were also small decryption units, working both on Enigma and other forms of coded messages. In Heliopolis, just outside Cairo, the Combined Middle East cipher operation was based in a disused museum. As the war progressed, the work of the listeners acquired a more mobile dimension: wireless operators out in the desert in specially adapted vans, working through insufferable

BELOW The Bletchley out-station at Kilindini, Mombasa, was based in a beautiful requisitioned 19th century school building. The cryptologists and Wrens worked on increasingly complex Japanese codes in large, airy school rooms and from there liaised with Washington and Melbourne.

the dizzying beauty and glamour of life there; the dances in fantastically luxurious hotels, the louche aristocratic ex-pats. She and others were witnesses to a world that was very soon to disappear.

There were also small mobile units operating in Greece. When the Germans launched their invasion of 1941, the wireless operatives found themselves in a desperate race both to stay ahead of the enemy, and also to protect their secret equipment. This then applied all over again with the invasion of Crete. For a few, such as Edgar Harrison, evacuation was an extremely close-run thing, and involved days of hiding out in caves before it was possible to mount a sea rescue.

In 1942, the 'Y' station on Singapore was in even greater jeopardy. One Wren recalled how even beforehand, it was never the easiest posting. The humidity and temperature were frequently unbearable, and the sweat ran into her shoes. And despite their round-the-clock monitoring, it was difficult for them to know exactly what the enemy was planning next – not because of a failure in codebreaking, but because the Japanese tended to use abstract keywords for their operations, an obstacle which no

heat and cold eerie nights, shaking scorpions out of their boots. They tuned in to Rommel's forces and at one point they were – triumphantly – relaying so much information back to Bletchley that the British knew more about the German supply line situation than Rommel himself.

As the war in the Middle East went on, increasing numbers of female operatives, such as the WAAF Eileen Clayton, were posted to listening stations closer and closer to the front line – to the horror of some senior commanders. Clayton in fact had a dramatic war not only in North Africa (where she met General Eisenhower) but also on the besieged island of Malta where, on the way back from one night shift, she was strafed by a Stuka. This was on her 24th birthday, and she was remarkably good-humoured about it. Other women, such as Cherrie Ballantine, who had been sent from Bletchley Park to Cairo in 1940, recalled

TOP Long after the gruelling siege is over, 'Y' Service operatives gather on the cliffs of Malta.

RIGHT Taking leave in the Cocos (Keeling) Islands – boat trips out into the azure sea to watch manta rays and sharks.

ABOVE Unlike severely rationed Britain, those working in Colombo had unlimited access to delicious tropical fruit –including much sought-after pineapple and bananas.

MESSAGE FORM

G.S.S.	**MESSAGE FORM**	MESSAGE SERIAL No.	

NAME	Braun Can	DATE 17-7-45	T O	CALL RAD
		T I M E	BEGINS 2935 G.M.T.	FREQUENCY 3·0
FILE No. V/NW/·85			ENDS G.M.T.	R.S.T. 5·9
		SERVICE No. 7/23	F R O M	CALL X25
		—OR—		FREQUENCY 6870
		G.S. BAND ....kc/s to...... kc/s		R.S.T.

PREAMBLE   CT XZ 184 = 1/60

IVPDT	EVFTK	COELP	Z4DDY
MSBFK	OROSE	YWRCK	GAISE
KXQHL	SLVGC	IQWF	DVUQY
WUVLG	VLULL	AICMS	ZUPWC
MRLTZ	IH--T	J----	CGURT
PVZRN	DNLKR	ZOPAT	GRDG-
NDYTG	LPNES	RCIPN	HIOVI
SKAWC	MACNP	SKFVA	DAWPK
DMFHS	NSEFE	ULOGS	VPZIT
VYRGH	VJABJ	FAXXC	BLRRS
WMOVT	BNABG	GRADX	MVFSC
SCLFT	QSTTN	NTNBR	OGJXQ
GBVNL	GFDWD	ASJSK	ZZTTR
GD-TT	VROXF	GNPJY	XPLNS
SGTRO	BRBGX	XJBBT	TRXGH	AR

OBSERVATIONS OR NOTES

amount of codebreaking could ever surmount. When the invasion came, the 'Y' team and their cryptology experts only just managed to get out with mere hours to spare. Capture was unthinkable, and this applied equally to operatives in the Middle East and the Mediterranean: if, under torture, any hint of Bletchley Park's success had been disclosed, the consequences would have been incalculable. The operatives simply could not allow themselves to fall into enemy hands.

Wireless operators often came from a background in the Post Office. When the war broke out, some were too young to join up; but they honed their wireless skills against the day that the call-up came. Many young men were taken off to training centres based in requisitioned holiday camps. Remembered as being particularly chilly and uninviting was the Skegness branch of Butlins, Bob Hughes recalled how they slept in chalets, in double beds with thin boards down the middle – to stop recruits 'getting at one another' in the night. But it was so freezing cold that they got rid of the boards and slept close for warmth anyway. He also recalled how, after so many weeks of deeply immersive Morse training, enabling them to reach speeds of 30 words per minute, they were then deployed across the world. The contrast between grey Britain and the stark beauty of Alexandria or Sardinia was breathtaking. A few veterans – recruits who had never even seen a swimming pool before – recalled their delight at being able to plunge into the rich blue of the Mediterranean and the Red Sea.

The 'Y' Service was life-changing too. Many veteran Wrens were later to confess that, determined as they were to do their bit for the war effort, they were also keen to do so with work that was interesting and absorbing and made more demands of them than being cooks or drivers or mess waitresses. Some had an awareness of what was required for interception work, and made sure that they had learned the basics of Morse before their interviews. They were summoned before panels – many featuring unsmiling older women – and given intelligence and aptitude tests. Some women were recruited for their deftness in Morse; others for the range of their linguistic skills. Like the men, they were packed off to training centres. One, on the Isle of Man, was remembered with especial fondness by many veterans. The work was tough but the island seemed to be a cornucopia of foodstuffs – from fresh eggs to fish – that were severely rationed elsewhere. Other recruits were sent to Soberton Towers in Hampshire, remembered for its Malory Towers atmosphere.

But then came the real experience for so many of these women: embarking aboard troop ships, with only the faintest idea of where they were being sent. A few were dispatched to Mombasa on the coast of East Africa, where there was a base established in an old school-house, which was dealing with Japanese codes. A couple of Wrens, when they got leave, took the opportunity to climb Mount Kilimanjaro.

A great many other 'Y' Service operatives, women and men, endured gruelling voyages to be sent to HMS Anderson, a huge station outside Colombo in Ceylon. After the tension of a long voyage through U-boat infested waters, arrival was a relief. One veteran from Weybridge in Surrey recalled his wonder when looking out at the night sky and seeing 'millions of fireflies'. Meanwhile, women who had had to deal with nothing larger than money spiders suddenly found themselves in a world of snakes, lizards and outsize tarantulas – all of which they quickly adapted to with high good humour.

Out here, the wireless interceptors were listening in on the Japanese forces, in addition to tracking their shipping and submarines by means of Direction Finding. Veterans recall their speedy tutorials in the basics of Japanese language and culture, the better to help them relay intelligence back to Britain. And in the off-duty hours, Colombo was really quite the place to be. The swimming was excellent, the food a source of terrific pleasure after the meagre and limited diet back home; and the night-life was extraordinarily exotic, especially to women aged 18 or 19 who had never before even left their home towns. And aside from several bombing raids in 1941, the atmosphere was relatively tranquil. The only regular disturbances, especially for women working alone on night shifts in huts fretted with palms, were spectacular thunderstorms. They might have been glorious to watch but when sitting with earphones clamped on, trying to

LEFT Sailor and Morse specialist Peter Budd was aged 19 when he was sent out first to Colombo, and then the remote Cocos Islands. He managed to take camera film with him courtesy of his girlfriend's chemist father.

OPPOSITE Budd was listening in on enemy communications, and also tracking submarines. Those stationed on the island had to translate and transcribe coded messages from Morse at very high speeds. He recalled that night shifts on a lonely island could be eerie; and there was constant watchfulness in case of a Japanese attack.

listen to enemy frequencies, the crackling and the interference was sometimes agonising. Many Wrens found after the war that their hearing had been permanently damaged.

For some of these young people, the work opened up vistas they could never before have imagined. The experiences of 19-year-old Peter Budd, a Bristol boy who had previously considered Calais as distant as Timbuktu, left an indelible mark – he was sent to the absurdly remote Cocos Islands in the middle of the Indian Ocean, some 2,000 miles from any mainland. He and 18 other colleagues, who were looked after by a tiny community of Malay people, conducted their wireless work in a place that he considered heaven: fine white sand, mesmerising amethyst sea, manta rays, beer and gramophone records on the beach. His 18 months there had an edge of the surreal: no one was allowed to know where on the planet he was, not even his parents. The

NAME				Day	Month	Year	**GROUP** OR **G.S. BAND**		CENTRE		Sheet No.
FILE No. V/HN/353				9	12	41			kc/s to	kc/s	
							SIGNALS HEARD, ETC.				Mes-sage Serial No.
Dial Read'g	KC/S	R.S.T.	CALL AS SENT	TIME G.M.T.			N.B. (I) ENTER PREAMBLE AND FIRST GROUP OF TEXT. (II) WHEN ON A.W. ENTER SERVICE NUMBER. (III) ALL OBSERVATIONS OR NOTES TO BE IN BRACKETS.				
							* CONTROL		* ANSWER		
	5400	438	CZE de	1700			QSA∅ PSE CALL = K =SRI QSA∅ QRX NEXT				
							NW 73 GB SK		WATCH PLEASE		
	5400	438	GGG	1800			NIL IIK ND 22ND 34 QRM (QRM BLOTTED OUT)				
	5200						QTC (LISTENED TILL 1815 BUT ND) STILL WANTED				
	4880		(WER de URK)	1815			QTC CT 935/71 = (VY HEAVY ATMOSPHERICS)				
							A OHLC VUBAK –NKUZ MH PXN LTUPK				
							XFGEL WOFYH RDZFZ RZAXP DFJZB				
COVERED THANKS							TYHNW OPLDU NECIW FSJGS QVYIG				
							DVDQX WBDMJ MHRWW NKLFW UFF-O				
							THZGQ OOVKW CZEHQ MWEKE HZ-ZM				
							ZQDD MIWF VXAOU KOVVW CNCXX				
	5190	429	DUF de				RPT W35 PSE QSY (Parts of this may be other				
	4900		URK				CT T---Fx Stations. I could hear about four)				
							QFK IIH APSY- OYIIR LCHUP FBJJL				
							YJHHO RIPBG WLYRY MMTUR OMIUQ				
							MFDQY EOVEG PQEZB IUVCU ADWNY				

* DELETE WHEN NOT APPLICABLE AND IGNORE CENTRAL DIVISION.   C484) 8,000 pads G.S.St.

location of the station was so sensitive, owing to its proximity to the Japanese, that it was even removed from official maps. To all intents and purposes, Budd and his colleagues were working on an island that didn't exist. Aside from the menace of lethal caterpillars that could cause total paralysis, and the occasional fright from a shark, these islands represented a paradise that he never found again.

Less exotic, but central to Bletchley's efforts, were the listening stations dotted all around the coast of Britain, from Dover to Wick. On the south coast, these stations, which ranged from the extensive base at Dover to more extemporised locations – cottages, a lighthouse, even an old caravan – were not only picking up encoded messages, but also the conversations of German pilots. In the early days of the war, before radar was properly working, these listeners were pretty much the human equivalent, relaying the conversations between pilots and controllers just seconds after they had happened. Speed and accuracy were key, and this is why the work required such young recruits. Veterans

recalled how some, only in their thirties, simply could not match the nimbleness and innate cheerfulness of their younger counterparts, and would burn out.

The German pilots were only too aware that they were being overheard, and they would sometimes address jokes and greetings to the invisible women who were listening in. This sometimes created a curious sort of intimacy. Some Wrens recalled the feeling of sickness when these high-spirited young pilots were eventually shot down out of the sky, and they were forced to listen to their final terrified cries.

Closer to home, the south coast of England was also a serious target: it was known as 'Hellfire Corner' with good reason. A couple of Wrens remembered how they would pick up messages from across the Channel about the launch of missiles only, just seconds later, to realise the missiles were heading in their direction. In Scarborough, the Wrens were doing the vital work of tracking and monitoring U-boats, and relaying the encoded messages back to Bletchley Park. In the beautiful Suffolk seaside town of

Southwold, meanwhile, the men and women of the 'Y' station there found that life alternated between pleasant tranquillity and bombardment, either from German shipping or from enemy bombers dropping the last of their explosives on the way back after missions.

At 19th-century Beaumanor Hall in Leicestershire, 'Y' Service operatives worked round the clock in huts, rather like their Bletchley counterparts, although the atmosphere was less happy. The task was more perspiration than inspiration; the effort of staying awake on quiet night shifts was so great that listeners would occasionally have to jab their wrists with lit cigarettes. For those few who didn't smoke, the tobacco fug was almost unendurable. Yet the work was pivotal; the material that Beaumanor was relaying to Bletchley was remarkable in its pinpoint accuracy and speed. A few miles away from Bletchley at Chicksands Priory there were some personnel difficulties, caused chiefly by the fact that so many of the young women working there had never before left home, and were finding it tricky

to adjust to a working life filled with abstract dots and dashes, faint frequencies, and no clue whatsoever about the effect or the importance of their tasks. One young woman punched her superior officer out cold; a psychiatrist drafted in to write a report about the entire establishment found it seething with stress, and wondered if there might not be some way, outside of the Official Secrets Act, of letting the women know how crucial their roles were.

Some women were drafted to the most northern Scottish bases. There was a tremendous amount of curiosity on both sides, with the Scottish girls asking them about the impossible pace of London life, and the English women adjusting to this bleak world of gorse and knife-sharp winds. As with Bletchley, it seems that the cure-all for any malaise was a good dance, and there were a great many in the far north. Scarborough too became renowned for the quality of its off-duty life. Down south in Hampshire, at the on-shore base HMS Flowerdown, the wireless-intercept Wrens lived for their nights out, particularly with the advent of

RIGHT A 1930s glimpse of the extent of the Bletchley stables; by the time Alan Turing started work in adjacent offices, they had been cleared.

BELOW The courtyard is still there today, near the entrance of the building termed 'the Cottage', where senior codebreaker Dillwyn Knox worked.

American soldiers. They would pick the Wrens up in trucks and motor through the countryside around Winchester. Though many veterans insist that this really was a far more innocent age and that, in general, they would never have dared to get into serious relationships with these smooth interlopers, obviously there were exceptions to this. In Bletchley Park alone, there were a couple of notable long-term pairings between English women and American codebreakers. Some wireless-intercept Wrens and GIs – those who had not had affairs – kept their platonic relationships alive long after the war.

Intelligence analysts had another fantastically useful, top-secret army – the VIs, or Voluntary Interceptors. Sixteen-year-old Ray Fautley was madly enthusiastic about the science of radio from his early boyhood and worked for Marconi. One evening in 1941, at home with his parents, he received a visit from the Man From The Ministry. Would young Mr Fautley be interested in carrying out highly confidential war work? Would he ever! Ray was required to install a large receiver in his parents' front parlour, hidden within a bureau. And when he got home each evening, he would be expected to do two hours' interception work, tuning in to prescribed frequencies. Having noted down all the Enigma-encoded Morse traffic on specially provided stationery, he then had to send the results, in a special sealed envelope, to PO Box 25 Barnet. The work was so secret not even his parents were allowed to know what he was doing. On one occasion, his girlfriend walked in on him with the receiver and instantly assumed he was a spy.

His interceptions – and those of some 1,500 volunteers right the way across the country – ended up in a handsome villa in north London, where Lord Sandhurst, Hugh Trevor-Roper and their team would subject all the traffic to detailed analysis and by doing so were able to build up a remarkably detailed portrait of the Abwehr (German military intelligence) and its various activities worldwide.

ABOVE AND RIGHT Local fauna – from reptiles to mosquitos – could be trying but Wrens such as these women Algeria (right) and Colombo (above) soon acclimatised.

For a great many men in the 'Y' Service – either out in the field with innovative equipment or back at base working with quicksilver speed and accuracy – satisfaction came from demonstrating their prowess with the technology; the brain-scrambling ability to translate Morse coming in through one ear while tracking directions and positions with the signals came through the other. The job needed intelligence and initiative, but more than

LEFT The 'Y' Service work was exacting but much sought after. Many young women purposefully learnt Morse in order to be recruited. Nor did they lose the skill in the years after.

this: as some veterans recalled, it saved many of the recruits coming through from getting stuck with more routine mechanical or maintenance roles. This was wartime work that – although top secret, and intended to remain so for many years – would actually stand them in good stead for a post-war world of ever-increasing electronic innovation. For the women, the 'Y' Service was a boon on many levels: the chance to take on a job that had a tangible impact – even if the work was secret, congratulations would still filter through if their interceptions had helped save a convoy. Then there was the extra satisfaction of doing work that was formerly considered to be purely the domain of men. For veterans who recalled mugging up on Morse code before being called up – or getting brothers and fathers and uncles to teach them – the effort and the hard work that followed was very much worth it. Added to this was an element that caused many veterans to laugh when recalling: the Wrens' uniform itself. It

was considered by some distance to be the most glamorous of all the service options available. Certainly when they were all lined up on parade in the tropical light of Colombo, it was clear to see they wore these uniforms with a combination of pride and pleasure. For the Wrens, as for so many of the Bletchley codebreakers back in England, the war had opened up vistas and possibilities that afterwards would dramatically influence the course of their lives. It is only really now that the importance of their work is finally being properly celebrated.

RIGHT A fitting memorial at the National Memorial Arboretum to the brilliant work done by thousands of young Wrens and sailors at intercepting the enemy's every message.

DEDICATED TO THE MEN AND WOMEN OF

THE "Y" SERVICES

WHO MAINTAIN A CONSTANT SILENT WATCH ON THE ENEMIES OF THEIR COUNTRY

THEIR PAST AND CONTINUING CONTRIBUTION TO BRITAIN'S OPERATIONAL SUCCESS IN PEACE AND WAR CAN NEVER BE TOLD IN FULL

APOLLO
THEATRE

TOBY ROWLAND LTD.

presents

SUMMERTIME

A new Comedy by UGO BETTI
English Version by HENRY REED

PROGRAMME
SIXPENCE

9

Bletchley Park's Famous Faces

LEFT Actress and Bletchley recruit Dorothy Hyson, seen here with co-star George Formby in *Spare A Copper* (1940). It was rumoured that Formby tried to seduce her. She also starred opposite Boris Karloff in *The Ghoul* (1933).

GIVEN THE FREEWHEELING ETHOS OF BLETCHLEY PARK, IT WAS ONLY TO BE EXPECTED THAT THE RECRUITMENT NET EVENTUALLY SPREAD RATHER WIDER THAN OXBRIDGE MATHEMATICIANS. AS THE PARK GREW, SO TOO DID THE RANGE OF CODEBREAKERS, AND THE DISCIPLINES FROM WHICH THEY WERE DRAWN. A TALENT FOR LINGUISTICS, AND EVEN THE VERY STRUCTURE OF LANGUAGE ITSELF, WAS A QUALIFICATION. AND SO IT WAS THAT AMONG THE CALCULUS EXPERTS AND THE CHESS CHAMPIONS, THERE SOON APPEARED POETS, NOVELISTS, AND YOUNG POLITICIANS, TOO. AS WE HAVE SEEN, THERE ALSO SEEMED TO BE A STRONG PREDILECTION TOWARDS MUSICIANS AND ACTORS. SOME WHO WORKED AT BLETCHLEY WERE ALREADY VERY WELL KNOWN; OTHERS WOULD GO ON LATER TO BECOME HIGHLY PROMINENT AND INFLUENTIAL PUBLIC FIGURES.

Many veterans, for instance, recalled with fondness Baron Jenkins of Hillhead – Roy Jenkins when he was drafted into Bletchley Park in 1943. Born in Wales in 1920, Jenkins had already made an impact at Balliol College, Oxford, by pulling off a First in Politics, Philosophy and Economics. He had a brilliant mind but one that was not best suited to the particular discipline of codebreaking, with its emphasis on mathematical flair, along with the patience to run through endless combinations during the middle of the night. Given these drawbacks, Jenkins acquitted himself as best he could, apart from one period of a few weeks when, by his own admission, he was almost completely useless. He had originally been called up in 1942 to serve with the West Somerset yeomanry; there is a suggestion that he was pulled into Bletchley's orbit via the influence of A. D. Lindsay, the Master of Balliol College.

After the War, Jenkins immediately gravitated towards politics. He won the London seat of Southwark Central in 1948 and became for a while the youngest face in the Commons. Two years later, he shifted to the slightly more stable seat of Stechford in the Midlands. Following a long spell in opposition, and then Harold Wilson's 1964 election victory, Jenkins was appointed Home Secretary in 1965 and Chancellor in 1967. It was in the former post that he became arguably the most influential politician of

OPPOSITE Lord Jenkins of Hillhead – pictured when he was Labour Home Secretary in 1968 – was wry and modest about his time at Bletchley, and about how much (or how little) he achieved when working on the Tunny codes.

LEFT The Master of Balliol, Oxford, and University vice chancellor A.D. Lindsay. Although not at Bletchley Park himself, this celebrated academic steered a number of young recruits – including Roy Jenkins – towards the codebreaking effort.

RIGHT One of Bletchley's more glamorous recruits was the film and theatre actress Dorothy Hyson (right), seen here co-starring with Gracie Fields in *Sing As We Go* (1934), a giant hit that year.

his generation. As with all his former colleagues at Bletchley, he kept quiet about his own role for many decades afterwards, though he frequently ran into former codebreaking colleagues in Whitehall and at cocktail parties.

Even more discreet was the West End actress Dorothy Hyson, who worked in Hut 8. Unlike Jenkins, she was already very famous; a household name in fact. The daughter of the actress Dorothy Dickson, Hyson was on the stage from an early age and specialised in light comedies and dramas. In the 1930s, she made the leap to film. She starred alongside Gracie Fields in the phenomenally successful Sing As We Go and was the co-star to popular comedian George Formby in Spare A Copper. She was married to the actor Robert Douglas but had met another actor, Anthony Quayle, on stage in the 1930s when they had appeared together in A Midsummer Night's Dream. There was an instant attraction, and by the time she was working at Bletchley they were having an affair. It was, by necessity and for reasons of security, a long-distance relationship. Quayle was part of the elite Special Operations Executive, ordered by Churchill to set Europe ablaze in operations ranging from sabotage to provoking local uprisings. This must have taken an extraordinary amount of courage; and yet what Quayle also recalled from his war years were his visits to Bletchley Park in order to see Hyson. He remembered that he watched Dorothy and her colleagues emerge from their huts after an all-night shift, looking pale and gaunt. He had no idea of the sort of work they were doing but it was clear that it was incredibly intense. After the War, Hyson and Quayle married. For a time, she joined John Gielgud's Haymarket Theatre Company, then she quietly gave that up in order to concentrate on family life. Having spent so much of her time in the world of theatre, the rather different theatrics to be witnessed at Bletchley must have left her bemused.

Of the senior directorate of Bletchley Park, one who had quite a high social profile was the veteran codebreaker Nigel de Grey. It was he, together with a colleague in Whitehall's Room 40, who had broken the codes that led to the revelation of the Zimmerman Telegram of 1917. This telegram, from a German foreign minister to his opposite number in Mexico, urging that they form an alliance against America, was the catalyst for bringing the US into World War One. Careful steps were taken to ensure the Germans believed that the telegram had been captured in Mexico, as opposed to having had their cable telegraphy intercepted and decoded. After the War, Old Etonian de Grey (born in 1886) went on to head up the Medici Society, purveyors of Old Master prints, and he was a familiar figure in London's art circles. He was noted at Bletchley for a certain theatricality of dress sense; as it happened, he was an enthusiastic actor, and a key player with the amateur dramatic group The Old Stagers and Windsor Strollers. But after the War, a more serious business lay in store for him; he was one of the founding directors of the institution that would go on to become GCHQ.

The Park also had its fine share of poets; there was Frank ('FT') Prince, for instance, a South African-born writer and academic who in the early 1930s had had poems published in T. S. Eliot's influential magazine The Criterion. Despite this early boost, it took a long time for his work to attract more serious notice. He met his wife-to-be, Elizabeth Bush, at Bletchley, and one of his more enduring works, 'Soldiers Bathing', was written around this time. But it was never going to be easy for anyone to make any kind of a living as a poet; and after the end of his codebreaking duties, he went into academia, becoming a Professor of English at Southampton. It was only many years after this that his poetry began to pick up an enthusiastic and fashionable following. The same was partly true for Henry Reed. A brilliant pupil who had taught himself Greek, Reed came to Bletchley and worked in the Italian and Japanese sections. It was here that he wrote perhaps his most famous work, 'The Naming of Parts', inspired initially by the drill that a sergeant would give in handling weapons. Reed had to find supplementary means to make a living after Bletchley, and he became a successful radio playwright, creating the popular long-running character Hilda Tablet.

Perhaps the best known now of all the Bletchley poets was Vernon Watkins, who published The Lamp and the Veil, The Lady with the Unicorn and Cypress and Acacia. Before the War, he had supported himself by working in a bank. Unlike T. S. Eliot, he was pretty much forced to carry on working in a bank, describing himself as a very elderly cashier. And he might have

LEFT Their love affair was as secret as Bletchley itself – but after the War, Dorothy Hyson and actor Anthony Quayle (who was in the Special Operations Executive) were happily married for many years.

found a certain sort of freedom of thought at Bletchley that his otherwise deadening peacetime routine could never have afforded him. While there, he met and married Gwendoline Davies. After Bletchley, he returned to Lloyds Bank and stayed there until his retirement in 1966. He died a year later, and it was only posthumously that his poetic reputation grew and was cemented. Of these poets, one might imagine that their ability to wrestle

with the language, to sculpt it into the shapes they wanted, also gave them a different way of approaching the seemingly intractable chaos of the five-letter groups; a way perhaps of being able to detect glimmers of structure in them.

As mentioned in chapter seven, a prominent figure at Bletchley Park was Angus Wilson, who had been working for the British Museum and who, immediately after the war, would find great literary success and indeed secure the rare ability to live off his writing. An acute and merciless social observer, Wilson's eye noted every nuance and layer of life at Bletchley. The Honourable Sarah Baring was rather impatient with him, and profoundly unsympathetic towards his depression; but what would Wilson have made of her – a one-time model for Cecil Beaton – and her beautiful society friend, Osla Benning? Wilson's post-war short stories dwelled on the cruelties of the class system. His own sense of middle-class gentility may have

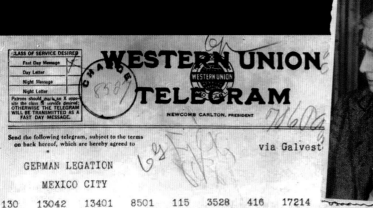

ABOVE Nigel de Grey, who was partly responsible for the intelligence gained from the Zimmerman Telegram, worked at Bletchley within the directorate, and inspired a great deal of awe among younger subordinates. After the war, he was instrumental in setting up the new GCHQ.

LEFT The 1917 Zimmerman Telegram – the brilliant decryption of which brought the US into WWI.

APOLLO
THEATRE

TOBY ROWLAND LTD.

presents

SUMMERTIME

A new Comedy by UGO BETTI

English Version by HENRY REED

PROGRAMME
SIXPENCE

been rather fragile.

Many of Bletchley Park's women recruits went on to enjoy illustrious careers and it is certainly possible that their successes at the Park gave them the boost they needed to make headway in what was firmly a world where women were expected to be home-makers. Mavis Lever (later Mavis Batey) made her name, for instance, as a pioneering landscape historian, a very new field. Inspired by W. G. Hoskins, she went on to have many of her own books published. On top of this, she was a prominent and active figure in the rambling movement.

Another of the Park's great achievers was Miriam Rothschild, awarded the CBE in 1982 and made a Dame in 2000. Her background was perhaps one of the more unusual to be found at Bletchley. Born in 1908 into a branch of the famous banking family, Miriam developed an early passionate interest in zoology and became a formidable expert on many species, but particularly snails. In the 1930s she had worked hard to get as many Jewish children out of Germany and Austria as she could. The war brought her to Bletchley, with her fine linguistic skills and ear for German. It must have been odd for her working around the house; her own family had lived not far away and she had known and visited the Leons in the days when the place was a cheerful social hub. After the war, her passion for butterflies, moths and other insects led to her being made the first woman trustee of the Natural History Museum in South Kensington. She went on to

One of Bletchley Park's American luminaries was William (Bill) Bundy. Born in 1917, Bundy was drafted into the Signals Corp when the US entered the War in 1941, and clearly demonstrated some sharpness and intellect; by 1943, he was in Hut 6, working under Stuart Milner-Barry and in charge of the US contingent.

While in the higher echelons of government and intelligence the famed 'Special Relationship' was more often marked with suspicion, distrust and even naked dislike, at the codebreaking level there was a huge amount of mutual respect between the British and their American counterparts. Like Colonel Telford Taylor, Bundy fitted well into this society of tea-drinkers. He was very impressed

RIGHT William (Bill) Bundy, an American cryptologist at Bletchley, was lost in admiration for the absurd Englishness of the establishment. He later went on to become a White House insider, working for John F. Kennedy.

that, despite all British archetypes, Bletchley was a near-perfect meritocracy and that military rank took second place to intellectual ability. He was also impressed to see so many women in key roles. There was, he recalled, much shared laughter over national differences, as well as an understanding on the US side that the secrecy was not just part of a stereotypical British fetish. After the War, Bundy sat for the Bar and thereafter gravitated towards politics. In the 1960s, he became a special adviser to President John F. Kennedy and then, after the latter's assassination in 1963, was taken on by his successor Lyndon B. Johnson as Assistant Secretary of State. Bundy was in the State Department dealing with affairs in the East and was there as the US became sucked into the maelstrom that was Vietnam. After his time at the State Department he became a historian, and it was for his time at Bletchley Park that he had a special affection. 'Though I have done many interesting things and known many interesting people,' he said, a few years before his death in 2000, 'my work at Bletchley Park was the most satisfying of my career.'

There's little doubt that a great many veterans have felt the same. In the case of all these high-profile figures, it is

LEFT Dame Miriam Rothschild CBE, one of the Park's true polymaths, with a fantastic ear for language and an intense scientific curiosity about the natural world.

TO BE KEPT UNDER LOCK AND KEY AND NEVER TO BE REMOVED FROM THE OFFICE. THIS FORM IS TO BE USED FOR AIR INTELLIGENCE MESSAGES ONLY.

112 BLETCHLEY PARK: THE SECRET ARCHIVES

LEFT Wartime naval intelligence operative Ian Fleming was a regular visitor to Bletchley and was clearly inspired there. The 1957 007 novel *From Russia With Love* featured the 'Spektor' encryption machine.

BELOW US codebreaker General Telford Taylor – pictured here giving evidence at the 1946 Nuremberg Trials – was beguiled by the apparent lack of hierarchy at the Park and by the idea of young women like Mavis Lever taking charge.

interesting to speculate how much the work there helped to shape their lives and careers thereafter. Surely, having faced the seemingly impossible across so many all-night shifts, life outside in a time of peace would have seemed comparatively easy? There is also the element of secret knowledge and thereby secret satisfaction; to have known that you were part of such an extraordinary team, to know that the work you did had such a profound impact on the course of the War, must have bestowed a certain inner confidence. Naturally, in cases such as those of Roy Jenkins and Miriam Rothschild, it's also possible that Bletchley and the War were lengthy interruptions in careers and pursuits that would have happened regardless. And we might also expect that, given the exceptional nature of all the Bletchley codebreakers, it would have been odd if some had not gone on to achieve fame in their chosen paths.

Nor is this intended to detract from the achievements of those who quietly got on with their lives afterwards – building solid careers in the Civil Service, returning to teaching, and so on. As we will see in Chapter Twelve, the years spent at Bletchley Park left an indelible mark on all those who were there. For many – rather like William Bundy – it was an emotional high-water mark remembered with aching nostalgia.

RIGHT The bombing
of Coventry in 1940;
to this day, a source
of controversy about
whether the Bletchley
codebreakers had
advance warning.

Broken Codes and the Course of History

IF BLETCHLEY PARK HAD NOT EXISTED – OR IF THE CODEBREAKERS HAD SOMEHOW FAILED ENTIRELY – WHAT WOULD HAVE BEEN THE EFFECT UPON THE OUTCOME OF THE WAR? OBVIOUSLY SUCH QUESTIONS COME FREIGHTED WITH AN INFINITY OF VARIABLES TO BE CONSIDERED. BUT IT IS STILL POSSIBLE TO PAINT A CHILLING PICTURE. IMAGINE, FOR INSTANCE, A DESERT WAR IN WHICH ROMMEL PREVAILED – CRUSHING THE BRITISH FORCES AND FIRST REACHING CAIRO, AND THEN STRIKING ONWARDS TOWARDS THE RICH OILFIELDS OF ARABIA AND PERSIA. IF THE ALLIES HAD LOST EGYPT, IT IS CONCEIVABLE THAT THEIR INVASION OF FRANCE WOULD HAVE BEEN DELAYED UNTIL 1946, BY WHICH TIME THE NAZIS MIGHT WELL HAVE DEVELOPED WEAPONS MORE TERRIBLE THAN THE V-1 AND V-2 MISSILES AND ROCKETS.

Or if that is not enough, imagine this: the Atlantic convoys, and the predatory 'wolf packs' of U-boats: with no regular, reliable way of tracking them, lethal numbers of Allied ships, supplies and men, would have been consigned to the frozen deep, and Britain's supplies of food and fuel would have dropped to insupportable levels. Or even imagine Operation Overlord in 1944: think of how, without consistent reliable intelligence as to the positioning of the German divisions, the Allied landings in France could have resulted in an outright bloodbath, leaving the Nazis dominant and unbowed in Europe. Some, including President Eisenhower, believed that the work of Bletchley helped to shorten the War by two years. Professor Sir Harry Hinsley – who worked at Bletchley Park on the naval intelligence side of Enigma and later became the distinguished historian of British Intelligence – thought it might have been even more. It's fascinating now to examine all the different points in the history of World War Two where we can see that the secret, invisible intervention of the codebreakers had the most direct and dramatic effect.

OPPOSITE Coventry, 1940: despite industrial targets lying on the outskirts of the town, the Luftwaffe targeted the centre. Codebreaker Stuart Milner-Barry averred that until late in the day, it was assumed at Bletchley that that night's assault would be on London.

ABOVE Some stone from the ruthlessly levelled cathedral was still glowing molten some time after the attack.

BELOW Professor Sir Harry Hinsley, codebreaker and intelligence historian, who co-ordinated Bletchley's vital – and complex – contribution to D-Day.

There are the individual battles to be considered: flashpoints like the 1941 Battle of Cape Matapan. On that occasion, it was Mavis Lever's decryption of the Italian codes in 'The Cottage' at Bletchley Park with Dilly Knox that helped the British Navy to rout the Italian forces. Newmanry veteran Captain Jerry Roberts cited the 1943 Battle of Kursk, where the Russians successfully pulverised the German forces, as an example of Bletchley's far-reaching hand. For weeks before the battle, British intelligence had – with very great care so as not to give away the codebreaking secret – been passing invaluable information to the Soviets to do with German artillery, and the new materials that they were using for their tanks. Such advance information gave

ABOVE Triumph for the British at Cape Matapan in 1941 – thanks to 19 year old Mavis Batey's inspired decrypting of Italian codes. Admiral Cunningham visited Bletchley to deliver his personal thanks.

RIGHT There were times, like the Nazi invasion of Crete, 1941, when Bletchley Park provided advance intelligence which, while not bringing victory, at least enabled the British to make it a 'damaging exercise' for the Germans

the Soviets a chance to explore the potential weak spots in the attacking force.

Then there were times in 1942 when Field Marshal Rommel must have felt that he was in a boxing ring with the invisible man, receiving punches seemingly from nowhere. Curiously, the North African campaign saw the intelligence effort swinging like a pendulum. In the earlier stages, it was the Germans who had greater success in breaking through British cyphers, and listening in on British transmissions. But the Bletchley operation tightened up as the conflict intensified and – unusually – allowed top-security Enigma codebreaking work to be carried out away from the Park, within the Heliopolis section. There were glaring risks attached to this strategy. Indeed, on one particular day in 1942 which came to be known as 'Ash Friday', it looked as though Rommel's forces might have been on the point of breaking through, and the codebreakers very swiftly took all the material they had – all the papers, all the files – and made a vast bonfire so that any invaders would not be able to pick up a scrap of a sense of the work that they had been doing. The German push was a false alarm; and the hot Cairo air was filled with the grey floating embers of needlessly incinerated intelligence. Some veterans recalled the incident as a wry outbreak of black comedy. Nonetheless, throughout 1942, the Heliopolis unit, together with Bletchley back home, had the most fantastic successes in consistently unlocking the German Army Enigma ciphers. Indeed, wrote Professor Hinsley, these codebreakers provided '… more timely intelligence about more aspects of the enemy's activities than any force

enjoyed in any land campaign in the whole war'. Most spectacularly, the cryptologists were able – via Rommel's communications – to monitor closely the German supply lines, which were being devastated by Allied attacks on their shipping. They could tell, practically down to the last can of petrol, exactly how his divisions were fixed and when they were at their most vulnerable.

Then there was the constant tension of the Battle of the Atlantic; months and years in which the Germans sought to strangle the lifelines of an island nation. It was those in Hut 8 who were dealing with the challenge of Naval Enigma, and the reason this hut more than any other caused so much anxiety and bitter fighting in Whitehall was that so much depended on it not failing. This is why the authorities looked so askance at Alan Turing and his young team; the survival of the nation appeared to be in the hands

BELOW LEFT The 1943 Battle of Kursk in Russia was World War Two's largest tank engagement; the Russians received some crucial intelligence about German armaments from Bletchley beforehand, which helped swing the battle for them.

BELOW 'I can remember myself breaking messages about Kursk,' recalled Lorenz machine codebreaker Captain Jerry Roberts. 'We were able to warn the Russians that it was going to be a pincer movement and what tank units would be used.'

of abstruse, abstract disorganised mathematicians who could not even explain themselves in plain English. Were they really capable of breaking those Naval Enigma codes? Without being able to pinpoint positions and routes, there was very little that Allied shipping could do against the threat of the U-boats. Thanks to the complexities of that Enigma system, it took an agonisingly long time before any breakthrough could be made. When it came, though, in mid-1941, the result was instantaneous. 'At a time when the British anti-submarine defences were woefully weak and merchant shipping woefully scarce,' wrote Professor Hinsley, 'the use of decrypts to route convoys away from the U-boat patrols had a dramatic effect on the scale of the U-boats' depredation.'

The team in Hut 8 had been given a quantum boost by a brilliant cipher coup in May 1941. First there was the capture of the weather ship *München* – the crew managed to hurl their Enigma machine overboard but some crucial folders containing information on Enigma settings were overlooked. Then two days later came the dramatic attack upon the submarine *U-110* to the south of Iceland which was boarded by a party from HMS *Bulldog*; despite earlier efforts by U-boat captain Lieutenant Commander Lemp to destroy sensitive material, the sailors moving through the now empty and dark submarine took as much of the boat's equipment as they could; and in among their haul was a prize the significance of which they would have had little idea: an Enigma machine and cipher books. Although this didn't quite mean that the Naval Enigma team would be able to unlock codes at will,

ABOVE Colin Grazier, with Lieutenant Tony Fasson, swam to the *U-559* and salvaged the prize, handing Enigma material to 16-year-old Tommy Brown – but Grazier and Fasson paid with their lives. They were posthumously awarded the George Cross.

OPPOSITE TOP In both World Wars, the Germans were keen to use their submarines in propaganda – this poster was for an early film called *The Enchanted Circle*, a phrase actually stolen from Winston Churchill. Goebbels arranged for newsreels of U-boats returning triumphant to ports, while Bletchley desperately sought to crack their codes.

LEFT The U-boat menace to the convoys was made all the starker by the introduction in 1942 of an even more complex Enigma coding system; Admiral Dönitz, seen here greeting U-boat servicemen, had felt some disquiet about security.

BOTTOM LEFT Churchill said that the Battle of the Atlantic and the threat of the U-boats caused him the greatest anxiety; it was also the cause of terrific pressure at Bletchley as codebreakers sought to crack the German Naval codes. Here convoy PQ18 is attacked en route to aid Soviet shipping in 1942.

the haul enabled them to take invaluable shortcuts into regular decryptions. Incidentally, as we will see in chapter fourteen, this *U-110* pinch became the source of some controversy 60 years later when Hollywood grabbed the story and transformed it into a tale of American heroism.

At the start of 1942, Hut 8 faced fresh disaster when Admiral Dönitz ramped up the complexity of Naval Enigma by adding a fourth rotor: the decrypts dried up completely and did so for an appalling few months.

It was only thanks to a tremendous act of sacrifice that the impasse was broken. In late October 1942, on one pitch-dark night, the German *U-559* submarine was hit off the coast of Egypt. Able Seaman Colin Grazier and First Lieutenant Tony Fasson of HMS *Petard* swam naked through the black waters to get into the sinking vessel in order to retrieve any secret material there might have been on board. With terrific bravery — clambering aboard a vessel that was obviously sinking fast — they managed to get down into the freezing darkness, then find and pass water-proofed Enigma codebooks back to canteen assistant Tommy Brown. But then, now knee-deep in water, they also tried to haul equipment out of that blackness — and they were suddenly too late to escape as the submarine finally plunged. They were taken with it. Their courageous action, however, was almost beyond value: those codebooks were the Short Weather Cipher and the Short

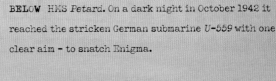

BELOW HMS *Petard*. On a dark night in October 1942 it reached the stricken German submarine *U-559* with one clear aim – to snatch Enigma.

Signal Book. It took just over three weeks to get them back to Bletchley. And instantly the codebreakers saw the treasure they had – these books in essence gave them an express route into unlocking the four-letter indicators, and thence each day's Enigma setting. Hut 8 got the books on 13 December 1942. Within just one hour of their first decrypts flowing through, intercepts of U-boat signals were sent through to the Admiralty, enabling them to instantly pinpoint the positions of fifteen U-boats. From that point on, an almost unquantifiable number of lives and vessels were saved as a result. Both men were posthumously awarded the George Cross, and they are commemorated annually in their home towns of Tamworth and Jedburgh. Tommy Brown, who survived (but sadly died in 1945), was awarded the George Medal. A little later, this and a couple of other code breakthroughs 'so changed the balance of power in the Atlantic,' wrote veteran Ralph Bennett, 'that the whole future course of the War in Europe may have hung upon it.'

In the earliest stages of the War, when the cryptographers were still trying to establish some kind of foothold into all the different Enigma codes, from the Army to the Luftwaffe, results

ABOVE Lieutenant Tony Fasson who helped change the course of the War

TOP HMS *Petard*'s young canteen assistant Tommy Brown. The bravery of Fasson and Brown on that dark night turned Bletchley's fortunes; and Tommy Brown was also awarded the George Medal for his crucial role.

ABOVE RIGHT The George Medal belonging to Tony Fasson which was donated by his family to the National Museum of Scotland.

LEFT The Enigma machine out in the field – battery-powered, and with two operators. Each different branch of the German military operation had its own version of Enigma and its coding combinations.

were more sporadic; even though, for instance, Bletchley had managed to penetrate the Luftwaffe Red code by the spring of 1940, the decrypts were still only of limited use throughout the Norway campaign and the Battle of Britain; in the case of the latter, intelligence gleaned from aerial reconnaissance and from the 'Y' Service listening posts dotted around the south coast was more effective. Those Bletchley out-stations – those Wrens and WAAFS instantly relaying conversations from German pilots – were in essence a sort of human radar.

But when the codebreakers started unlocking all the other codes, the flood of traffic and intelligence through Bletchley was

TO BE KEPT UNDER LOCK AND KEY AND NEVER TO BE REMOVED FROM THE OFFICE. THIS FORM IS TO BE USED FOR AIR INTELLIGENCE MESSAGES ONLY

122 BLETCHLEY PARK: THE SECRET ARCHIVES

awe-inspiring. At its peak in the later years of the War, it was breaking and translating and relaying to intelligence many thousands of messages a day. Even by 1941, this cottage industry was starting to hit industrial scales of production. The sinking of the *Bismarck* in 1941 was a brilliant early (and obviously top-secret) illustration of what the cryptographers could do. The *Bismarck,* sailing out from Bergen in Norway, had just sunk HMS *Hood*, with the loss of thousands of lives; and Bletchley pinpointed Luftwaffe Enigma messages that revealed plans to give the *Bismarck* air cover. There was another contribution – a sharp observation by Keith Batey in Hut 6. A German Air Officer in the Mediterranean had sent a

message to a colleague asking for the whereabouts of the *Bismarck* because the officer had a close relative on board the ship. The response duly came that she was sailing for France. The hunt for the *Bismarck* had also been joined by effective aerial reconnaissance and other intelligence. But the fact that Bletchley was so alert to the smallest and most random seeming of messages just showed what a formidable institution it was becoming.

There were also controversies – a belief that Bletchley had to cover up its own amazing successes at any cost, no matter how terrible – that continue to this day, the bombing of Coventry being one of the most vivid examples. The theory, still believed by many, is that the codebreakers had decrypted messages indicating that the city was to be targeted that terrible night in November 1940, and if Churchill had ordered the centre to be evacuated, that would have told the Germans that their secret messages had been

122

```
TO I D 8 G                    ZTP/1054
FROM GERMAN NAVAL SECTION G C AND C S

110/4595 KC/S              TO: 0025/27/5/41
          TOO 0153
TO FLEET W 70
ENEMY REPORT:
TO C IN C AFLOAT:
I THANK YOU IN THE NAME OF THE ENTIRE GERMAN PEOPLE.  ADOLF
HITLER
TO THE CREW OF THE BATTLESHIP BISMARCK:
ALL GERMANY IS WITH YOU.  ALL THAT CAN STILL BE DONE, WILL BE
DONE.  YOUR DEVOTION TO DUTY WILL FORTIFY OUR PEOPLE IN THEIR
STRUGGLE FOR EXISTENCE.  ADOLF HITLER.

TOO 2229/29/5/41+++AGT+++
```

LEFT An extraordinary decrypt: a pronouncement from Hitler addressed to the crew of the German battleship *Bismarck* on the day it was sunk. The vessel was finally tracked down thanks to the codebreakers.

RIGHT The sinking of the German battleship *Bismarck* in 1941 was a fantastic national morale boost – but it also lifted spirits at Bletchley Park, where the codebreakers had been invaluable in the effort to hunt it down.

read. And this in turn would result in them catastrophically increasing the complexity of their codes. So the city had to be sacrificed in that vast and searing inferno. But against this theory are the facts: there had indeed been messages about the forthcoming raid, but they referred to a mission known only by the term 'Korn'. This was beyond cryptology – it was an indecipherable key-word known only to a very few. And even by late afternoon on the day of the raid, just hours before the bombers came over, there was still uncertainty at Bletchley and in Whitehall as to whether the target would be London, Birmingham, Derby or Coventry. There was very little that anyone could have done.

There is an even more lurid theory that Bletchley so successfully penetrated the Japanese codes in late 1941 that it knew about the forthcoming attack on the US base Pearl Harbor, and that Churchill forbade anyone to pass the intelligence on because he was desperate for the Americans to come into

the War, and only an assault of this scale would make that happen. Again, it seems highly improbable; not least because British codebreakers in the Far East in 1942 utterly failed to interpret the Japanese intention to take Singapore. Rather like the Coventry episode, codes in this case had been successfully broken – but the Japanese used such specialised and abstract terms for their operations that no one could have hoped to have known what they were referring to.

ABOVE The Allied North African campaign was greatly boosted by the swift decryptions of the Bletchley out-station team on the outskirts of Cairo. Here the El Alamein bell is rung at the El Alamein Club in Cairo to commemorate the end of the War in Europe

BELOW RIGHT Churchill in the desert; the codebreakers of the Combined Bureau Middle East worked in an old museum and saw a decadent pre-Nationalist Cairo of opulent nightclubs and grand hotels.

BELOW Victory in the desert; at El Alamein, 1942, Bletchley broke the Chaffinch key, and saw the crucial vulnerable points of Rommel's supply lines.

NR. No.		GR. No.			OFFICE SERIAL No.
DATE		TIME OF RECEIPT	TIME OF DESPATCH	SYSTEM	

TO :

FROM :

SENDERS No.

PAGE FOUR.   CX/MSS/T183/84 (CONTINUED).
————————   ————————————————

    ENEMY MINING FROM THE AIR REMAINED LIVELY WITH SCHWERPUNKT OFF SUBMARINE BASES, LEZARDRIEUX AND AGAINST CHANNEL ISLAND NARROWS. AGENTS' REPORTS, APART FROM A PLETHORA OF LANDING DATES WHICH MAINLY POINT TO THE FIRST HALF OF MAY, YIELDED NO SPECIAL INFORMATION.

    C. IN C. WEST APPRECIATES THE SITUATION AS FOLLOWS:

    INVASION-PREPARATIONS BY THE ANGLO-AMERICANS IN THE ENGLISH MOTHERLAND ARE COMPLETED. DESPITE THE FACT THAT VISUAL AND PHOTO RECCE HAS NOT YET BEEN ABLE TO INCLUDE THE WHOLE OF THE ENGLISH SOUTH COAST, THE OBSERVED CONCENTRATIONS OF LANDING SHIPPING SPACE, ESPECIALLY IN THE AREA NORTH OF THE ISLE OF WIGHT (PORTSMOUTH - SOUTHAMPTON), NEVERTHELESS GIVE A CLEAR PICTURE OF A MAIN CONCENTRATION DEFINING ITSELF IN THAT AREA. TONNAGE OF SHIPPING SPACE FOR LANDINGS WHICH HAS SO FAR BEEN OBSERVED CAN ? ASSUMED TO BE SUFFICIENT FOR 12 TO 13 DIVISIONS (WITHOUT HEAVY EQUIPMENT AND REAR ELEMENTS) FOR FAIRLY SHORT SEA-ROUTES. TAKEN ALTOGETHER, AND INCLUDING AN ESTIMATE OF THE CAPACITY OF THE OTHER ENGLISH SOUTH-COAST HARBOURS WHICH HAVE S

DISTRIBUTION :			
DEGREE OF PRIORITY	TIME OF ORIGIN	SIGNATURE OF ORIGINATOR. NOT TO BE T	

LEFT Through hundreds of live decrypts, as the D-Day landings took place, Bletchley was monitoring minute by minute the German reactions to Allied subterfuge. Intelligence was relayed direct to Churchill. This historic top secret Ultra decrypt from 1944 shows German high command observing (yet also being blindsided by) preparations for Operation Overlord, unaware that their communications and countering plans were being followed minutely by the Allies.

RIGHT The D-Day landings of 1944 might have failed, according to Professor Sir Harry Hinsley, were it not for 'precise and reliable' ULTRA intelligence.

W/T RED FORM

ORIGINATOR SIGNED JODL COL
GENERAL FOR ACTION GRAND ADMIRAL
DOENETZ GENERAL FIELD MARSHALL
KEITEL ACT OF MILITARY SURRENDER.
PARA ONE. WE THE UNDERSIGNED
...G BY AUTHORITY OF THE GENERAL
... COMMAND HEREBY SURRENDER
... -...Y TO THE SUPREME
... ...ED EXPEDITIONAR

There is no doubting that one of Bletchley Park's most spectacular triumphs was its contribution to Operation Overlord in 1944. The codebreakers joined with other intelligence departments in playing deadly serious games of bluff and counter-bluff. 'In wartime,' said Churchill, 'truth is so precious that she should always be attended by a bodyguard of lies.' The aim was to trick the Germans into anticipating that an invasion would be landing not on the beaches of Normandy but in the region of the Pas de Calais. The means was a phalanx of turned agents, false military manoeuvres and deceptive messages. And invisible behind all of this was Bletchley Park; in the run-up to D-Day, the Park's

LEFT The historic decrypt of May 1945 bringing news of Germany's surrender. As with all other hyper-sensitive information, those who intercepted the message were required to keep quiet

BELOW A chance, finally, to raise a glass. Codebreakers gather together to celebrate VE-Day – although for many of them, their work was to continue long after.

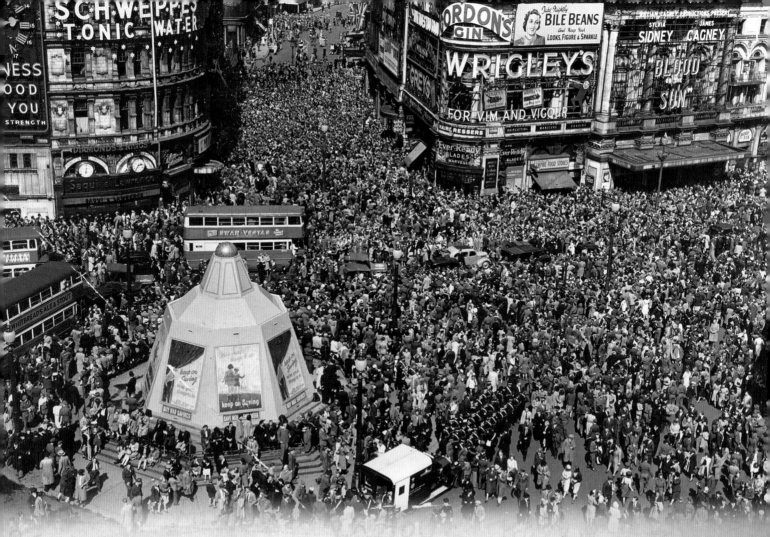

successful cracking of the Abwehr codes allowed them to know precisely what German intelligence was thinking, and this in turn helped British intelligence formulate further deceptions. The other crucial element for the planning of D-Day was knowing exactly the German military dispositions, and in this the codebreakers, by means of reading military, air force and intelligence keys, scored an uncanny triumph. Obviously the entire enterprise was still fraught with enormous hazard, but the codebreakers of Bletchley Park gave the Allied forces the closest thing they could get to a crystal

ball. Indeed, as Professor Hinsley observed many years later: 'It is a singular fact that before the expedition sailed, the Allied estimate of the number, identification and location of the enemy's divisions in the west, 58 in all, was accurate in all but two items.'

Towards the end of the War, traffic coming through Bletchley Park decreased significantly; the German forces, now pushed back on the defensive, were using landlines more and radio less; as a result, fewer messages were being intercepted. The German High Command was still using Lorenz, though, which gave the Newmanry personnel plenty of 'Fish' material to work through. By the spring of 1945, they were listening to the Nazi hierarchy starting to disintegrate. Veterans of Bletchley – codebreakers, Wrens, ATS women – had vivid memories of VE Day, and of the news coming through. Up and down the country, women and

ABOVE As VE Day crowds celebrated, the codebreakers at Bletchley allowed themselves a more decorous evening of celebration.

LEFT St Pauls Cathedral, May 1945, bathed in light for the first time since 1939.

men in the 'Y' Service stations also recalled how they stepped out, blinking, from the last of their all-night listening shifts, and gazed at the flames of the celebratory bonfires that had been lit. Very few of these veterans would have a proper idea of the impact that their work had had; owing to deep secrecy, and compartmentalisation, right up until the end, such information was out of bounds. And so it was that their wars ended without them quite understanding how vital their contribution had been. A great many were not to know until decades later, when the Bletchley secret at last began to seep out. For some, it was already too late. And even now, the triumphs of Bletchley Park are difficult to quantify.

Now putting $\ell_\chi = 1$ for all χ we see that one member of
the series $\mu_1 \cdots \mu_{2b}$ is 1, for (E) is certainly
satisfied. I shall prove that th
s tisfy $|\mu| \leqslant 1$. We first pr
$\Sigma p_\chi \ell_i = 0$. This follows by mu
side by p_χ and summing. Sinc
we get

$$\sum_{\chi y} q_{\chi y} \ell_y = \sum p_\gamma \ell_i$$

which implies $\mu = 1$ or
satisfy (E) with $\mu \neq 1$. Th
$\Omega \ell_\sigma < 0$ for some σ,
for which $|\mu| > 1$ is real and
with $|\mu| > 1$; then the eige

$$\sum_\beta (Q^r)_{\chi\beta} (1 + \varepsilon(\ell_f$$

If $\varepsilon > 0$ has been chosen so
then the L.H.S. is positiv
matrix are positive, where
suitably chosen r , u
we may take it that ℓ_χ
must satisfy $\Sigma p_\chi \ell_i = 0$

THE HUT SIX STORY

BREAKING THE ENIGMA CODES

— GORDON WELCHMAN —

11

What the Codebreakers Did Next

LEFT Alan Turing (right) at the console of the Mark I computer at Manchester, 1951 – he is with two engineers from arms and electronics company Ferranti, which had been brought in by the government to explore the development of the computer, alongside Professor Max Newman's theoretical work.

Now putting $\ell_\alpha = 1$ for all α we see that one member of the series $\mu_1 - \mu_{2b}$ is 1, for (E) is certainly satisfied. I shall prove that the remaining eigenvalues satisfy $|\mu| < 1$. We first prove that if $\mu \neq 1$ then $\sum p_\alpha \ell_\alpha = 0$. This follows by multiplying (E) on each side by p_α and summing. Since $q_{\alpha\beta} = \dfrac{p_\alpha \beta}{T_\alpha}$ and $\sum_\alpha p_{\alpha\beta} = p_\beta$ we get

$$\sum_{\alpha\gamma} q_{\alpha\gamma} \ell_\gamma = \mu \sum p_\gamma \ell_\gamma = \mu \sum p_\alpha \ell_\alpha$$

which implies $\mu = 1$ or $\sum p_\alpha \ell_\alpha = 0$. ~~Let ℓ_α~~ ~~satisfy (E) with $\mu \neq 1$. Then $\sum p_\alpha \ell_\alpha = 0$ and therefore~~ ~~$\Re \ell_\sigma < 0$ for some σ~~. Next we show that each μ for which $|\mu| > 1$ is real and positive. Let ℓ_α satisfy (E) with $|\mu| > 1$; then the eigenvalue for $\bar{\ell}_\alpha$ is $\bar\mu$ and so

$$\sum_\beta (Q^r)_{\alpha\beta} \left(1 + \epsilon(\ell_\beta + \bar\ell_\beta)\right) = 1 + 2\epsilon \Re \mu^r \ell_\alpha$$

If $\epsilon > 0$ has been chosen so small that ~~xhexRxMxS~~ $\Re \epsilon \ell_\beta > -\frac{1}{2}$ all β then the L.H.S. is positive for the coefficients in the matrix are positive, whereas the R.H.S. is negative for suitably chosen r, unless $\ell_\alpha = 0$. If now $\mu > 1$ we may take it that ℓ_α is real for each α. As it must satisfy $\sum p_\alpha \ell_\alpha = 0$ it is negative for some α, but then

$$\sum_\beta (Q^r)_{\alpha\beta} \left(1 + \epsilon \ell_\beta\right) = 1 + \epsilon \mu^r \ell_\alpha$$

and if ~~xkm~~ ϵ is chosen so that ~~xkmxxk~~ $1 + \epsilon \ell_\beta > 0$ all β the L.H.S. is positive whereas the R.H.S. is negative for sufficiently large r. All the eigenvalues therefore satisfy $|\mu| \leq 1$.

FOR A GREAT MANY BRITONS, THE YEARS OF WORLD WAR TWO HAD AN INTENSITY THAT NOTHING AFTERWARDS EVER QUITE MATCHED. FOR THE YOUNG MEN POSTED TO DISTANT FOREIGN LANDS, OR FOR THE YOUNG WOMEN DRAFTED IN TO DO THE HEAVY INDUSTRIAL WORK BACK AT HOME, THERE WAS, AMID THE TRAUMA AND THE LOSS, A SENSE THAT NO DAY WAS EVER PREDICTABLE; THAT THERE COULD BE EMERGENCIES OR DISASTER AT ANY STAGE. ADDED TO THIS WAS THE DEEP FOCUS THAT CAME WITH THE FEELING THAT EVERY SINGLE INDIVIDUAL CONTRIBUTION COUNTED. FOR THE YOUNG PEOPLE OF BLETCHLEY, THAT DEEP WELL OF EXCITEMENT WAS ACCOMPANIED BY THE ADRENALINE-TRIGGER OF KNOWING ONE'S WORK WAS OF THE HIGHEST POSSIBLE SECURITY. AND WHEN THE WAR ENDED? HOW WOULD ONE EXPECT THESE HUNDREDS, THOUSANDS OF CODEBREAKERS AND WRENS AND LINGUISTS TO DEPRESSURISE AFTER YEARS OF WORKING AT MAXIMUM CONCENTRATION ON TASKS THAT MEANT THE DIFFERENCE BETWEEN LIFE AND DEATH FOR SO MANY?

As with the armed forces abroad, demobilisation at Bletchley Park was a gradual process. The Wrens and the WAAFs started to pack up as the intelligence traffic naturally dropped off – and they were eventually under orders to dismantle the bombe machines 'wire by wire, screw by screw', as one veteran recalled. After VE Day, the decryption work still went on – most obviously with the continuing focus on the Japanese codes. Nor did the end of the conflict in Europe mean that the work of codebreakers and listeners was over. Far from it. But the form it would take in peacetime was only an abstract concern to those who were

OPPOSITE Ian Turing's typewritten and annotated notes on 'The Applications of Probability to Cryptology'. His post-war work took him from Hanslope Park to the National Physical Laboratory to Manchester University.

eager to resume their normal civilian studies and careers. The winding down, the thinning out of hut personnel, led to some shift difficulties, as internal memos show: with fewer people around, it was harder for those who remained to be able to get Saturday mornings off for matters such as dental appointments.

Some of the codebreakers, particularly senior figures in the directorate, knew by this time that they would be staying on in whatever form the establishment was next to take. But for many of the others, marching out of those gates for the last time, back into a life of regular hours, and work not governed on a 24-hour cycle by an endless procession of nightmarishly random cyphers, that period of readjustment was tricky to negotiate. Normal life was a shade too normal; and on top of this, horizons had been widened.

One of the more illuminating post-war experiences was that of the young mathematician John Herivel, whose brilliant insight in

1940 led to the Park unlocking the Luftwaffe Enigma pretty much until 1945. Herivel left the Park and moved to Northern Ireland to teach. The experience was extremely unsatisfactory: he had to give it up when he realised that he had no control over the boys he was supposed to be teaching. To have moved from the collegiate anarchy of Bletchley to the uncongenial anarchy of school must have seemed at best a disappointment. Herivel then moved into academia, taking up a position as a lecturer in the History and Philosophy of Science at Queen's University Belfast. He also went on to write several books, including *Joseph Fournier: The Man and the Physicist*. Herivel's father had no idea what his son had done during the War, and the codebreaker was determined not to break the Official Secrets Act, no matter what the circumstances. On his deathbed, he accused his son of having 'achieved nothing' during the War. Heartbreakingly, he could not tell his dying father the truth.

BELOW Sir Stuart Milner-Barry said that reading German decrypts as they came through was like 'living with history'; after the War, he returned to his great passion of chess.

ABOVE After achieving so much in Hut 6, Keith Batey's post-war career ranged from the Foreign Office to aviation, to high academia.

Many of the codebreakers, drawn from Oxford and Cambridge, went on to pursue the careers that might have been expected from such graduates, as senior mandarins in the Civil Service. Stuart Milner-Barry, for instance, went on to become a Treasury Under-Secretary. This did not diminish his real passion, though and after his retirement, he took up a position rather closer to his heart – that of President of the British Chess Foundation. Milner-Barry, like Hugh Alexander, had been playing tournaments since childhood. At Bletchley, he was not the greatest mathematician and recalled that certain cryptological techniques and principles had to be explained to him several times over by Gordon Welchman. But he was a renowned strategic and lateral thinker, one of the Park's liveliest intellects. Again, we might see that a post-war working life – which involved coaxing the shattered and bankrupt British economy back into life – could have seemed staid. But there was also a sense here of a continuation of duty. The country had to be rebuilt. Both Oliver Lawn and Keith Batey also gravitated towards C.P. Snow's 'corridors of power', though not before Lawn had had a brief experience of academia. Batey joined the Foreign Office almost immediately after leaving Bletchley and was transferred to the High Commission in Ottawa. With no disrespect intended to the fine citizens of Canada, this posting – after the colour and urgency of the codebreaking life – must have seemed disconcertingly sedate. Indeed, during the War itself, Batey had itched for real action, and signed on to be a pilot – his desire was indulged, for a short time, before he was whisked back to codebreaking duties. After all that, the traditions and etiquette of the Foreign Office must at times have been grinding. By 1955, he changed direction and became Secretary of the Royal Aircraft Establishment at Farnborough – a much more enjoyable position that allowed him to pursue his fascination for aviation. Years later, he became Treasurer of Christ Church College, Oxford. Keith Batey was a terrific example of the formative power of a good grammar school – in his case, Carlisle. Although it would have been a slight stretch to describe Bletchley Park as a pure meritocracy, it is interesting that so many people with similar backgrounds to Batey flourished there, and went on to take their places in the Establishment. Another example is that

TO BE KEPT UNDER LOCK AND KEY AND NEVER TO BE REMOVED FROM THE OFFICE. THIS FORM IS TO BE USED FOR AIR INTELLIGENCE MESSAGES ONLY.

134 BLETCHLEY PARK: THE SECRET ARCHIVES

of Lord Briggs, known widely as the pioneering social historian Asa Briggs. He was educated at Keighley Grammar School in Yorkshire. His talents were spotted by an acute teacher and Briggs made it to Cambridge aged just seventeen. This was in 1937; he was told that they wanted him to take his degree before he was put into uniform. In 1943 – and by now in uniform – Briggs was recruited to Bletchley. Afterwards, he plunged back into academia: a fellowship at Worcester College, Oxford, then later the founding light behind the new University of Sussex in the early 1960s, and Chancellor of the Open University for many years. He also wrote many influential books. So Briggs clearly found satisfaction, plus also the right avenues for his tremendous energy. Not all his contemporaries were so fortunate.

For others, the comedown was somehow almost a matter of forgetting that Bletchley Park had ever happened. The Hon. Sarah Baring, who had worked with such dedication and zeal both at the Park and in a liaison role back at the Admiralty, found a completely different life on the very evening of VE Day; for it was then that she met William Waldorf Astor, the eldest son of Nancy Astor, and the man she was to marry. Sadly, the union did not last; they divorced in 1951, and although it was reasonably amicable, she cited the matter of the age difference (he was some

twelve years older than her). Nancy Astor apparently told her daughter-in-law: 'I think you're a goose to leave a millionaire!' But again, this was a time when the social landscape was shifting. In years beforehand, divorce was a matter for shame and scandal. At the dawn of the new Elizabethan age, mores were starting to become a little less rigid. She married again: Thomas Baring. And her son from her first marriage, the 4th Viscount Astor, just happens to be the stepfather of Samantha Cameron, the current Prime Minister's wife.

In those post-war years, Sarah Baring sometimes ran across old Bletchley colleagues at cocktail parties. She recalled that even as late as the mid-1970s, such encounters were accompanied perhaps with a smile and a wink, but absolutely no discussion; they were still bound by the Official Secrets Act. On top of this, she recalled, even if she had felt able to discuss her war work, people in general would not have wanted to listen. There came a point in those post-war years, she said, when it was considered a solecism to go on about the War itself. No one, she said, wanted to hear about it any more.

A few of the codebreakers elected to stay on, and they became the nucleus of a new organisation that was to coalesce in 1948 – GCHQ – as we shall see in chapter twelve. Others, though, headed out on to much more quotidian paths. Several senior cryptologists went to the John Lewis Partnership, a respectable retail firm. Chief among them was Gordon Welchman, who had done so much to streamline Bletchley's traffic analysis and turn it into the brilliantly sleek, fast and efficient outfit that it latterly became. To go from that to be a director of research for a chain of shops must have been particularly jarring: not because there is anything wrong with commercial business, but because it was such an unimaginable distance from the pressures and the satisfactions of wartime work. And clearly, Welchman could not settle – in 1948, he and his family moved to the United States.

BELOW Despite Max Newman's enthusiasm for computing, some veterans felt that excessive security meant that the UK got left behind. Research departments like this one at Manchester University, could not match the swift advances being made in the US.

OPPOSITE Jane Fawcett MBE, who became one of Britain's foremost architectural historians. She never felt entirely secure in Bletchley's blacked-out nocturnal streets and carried a hammer in her handbag. 'You never knew who you might meet,' she said.

—THE— HUT SIX STORY

BREAKING THE ENIGMA CODES

—GORDON WELCHMAN—

ABOVE Senior codebreaker Gordon Welchman's 1982 account – viewed dimly by the authorities – is still read as a key Bletchley text; there is a wonderful description of the day that Welchman met Churchill and the two men shared a conspiratorial joke.

TO BE KEPT UNDER LOCK AND KEY AND NEVER TO BE REMOVED FROM THE OFFICE. THIS FORM IS TO BE USED FOR AIR INTELLIGENCE MESSAGES ONLY.

136 BLETCHLEY PARK: THE SECRET ARCHIVES

He had had his introduction there during the War, visiting in 1943 to pool cryptology ideas. In those post-war years, he went back and headed straight for the new field of computing, the science of digital compiling. Though he was of course strictly bound by the Official Secrets Act, his experience must nonetheless have been extremely valuable. In 1962 he joined the American Mitre corporation, where his extremely sensitive role was to develop new secure systems for the US armed forces. This was the sort of work that required extremely stringent security clearances. And there he stayed, quite happily, until the early 1980s, when controversy struck. Observing the numbers of former colleagues – including Peter Calvocoressi – who were now writing books about Bletchley and the use of Ultra throughout the War, Welchman felt it was important to get his own memories down. This was not out of any unpatriotic desire to breach national security: rather, it was to ensure that the complexities and brilliant breakthroughs at the Park were faithfully and clearly rendered for future generations to study. That was not how the authorities in Britain or the US saw it, though, and when Welchman published The Hut Six Story in 1982, there were all sorts of pleas and appeals for him to desist.

Sadly, the Americans sided with the British: the result was that Welchman had his security clearance revoked. It is rather difficult now to see quite why the authorities were so agitated. Welchman added intriguing further details on the breaking of Enigma and, on a personal level, the odd splash of colour about the personalities and life at the Park. No one was betrayed, and by that time the general principle of Ultra, and the breaking of Enigma, was beginning to be widely known. But there are those who make something of a fetish of secrecy: to know something that no one else does confers a form of power. Welchman died not long afterwards, of cancer.

Others found that life after Bletchley lacked the intensity they had all grown so used to. Messenger girl Mimi Galilee, who had been promoted to clerical and secretarial work in

the Directorate, found herself acutely dissatisfied after the War. Living in London (and having worked for a time in Eastcote, the interim institution that followed Bletchley), she scratched around on unspectacular wages. Eventually, she ended up working for the BBC, at the time when it still had a studio and offices at Alexandra Palace in north London. In the course of her work there, and later for the World Service, she found herself encountering oddly familiar faces, though no one ever said anything. On one occasion in the 1970s, Mimi's BBC superior – who had himself had some dealings with intelligence – asked her where exactly she had been during the War. And still she wouldn't say, simply giving the stock response that she had been doing work for the Foreign Office. Her silence was part principle, and part habit; the War was a time, she recalled, when people everywhere learned to keep quiet, for fear of anything being of use to enemy agents. It might also be added that the BBC World Service in the 1970s, with its wide range of correspondents and contacts in unfriendly countries, might not have been the ideal place to be indiscreet during the Cold War.

For a great many women after Bletchley, there was an overwhelming social pressure to return to conventional roles as home-makers, mothers and housewives. Sheila Lawn, née MacKenzie, had been drawn to Bletchley from her university in Scotland. After the War, as her husband set about building a career, she was determined that her interrupted academic studies should not be allowed to peter out. She returned to Aberdeen University, then studied Social Science at Birmingham. The couple had children and she then went on to take a personnel job with London Transport. Unusually for the time, they employed an au pair. Other women, too, were determined that this post-war settlement would not see them relegated to second-class status. Jane Fawcett – who before Bletchley had studied ballet at Sadler's Wells under Ninette de Valois – went on to pursue quite another passion: architecture. In time, she was to head up the Victorian Society, previously chaired by Nikolaus Pevsner. And at a time, throughout the 1960s and 70s, when rapacious inner-city developers (unchallenged by apathetic politicians) were doing all they could to flatten Victorian structures and replace them with their own brutalist concrete money-spinners, it was campaigners like Jane Fawcett who were instrumental in saving so many landmarks such as St Pancras station. She was later to earn an MBE. She acknowledged the formative nature of her work at Bletchley – though in terms of aesthetics, she was never inspired by the town itself. 'It was a dump,' she recalled crisply.

For some of the veterans, it was the need to keep the secret from their children that sometimes caused unexpected moments of awkwardness. Mavis Batey recalled talking to her daughter one day about the Bodleian Library in Oxford, and her daughter mentioned how her job there involved working on Floor J. 'Oh,' said Mrs Batey, 'that's ten floors down.' Her daughter frowned and asked how her mother would have been able to work that out instantly. Mrs Batey laughed it off as an odd knack. It was actually years of working alongside Dilly Knox, and marrying letters up with numbers. And so life went on, though for the codebreakers and everyone else who had worked within those fences, there was another element of frustration: whereas all other branches of the services – from the regiments to the RAF to the Navy – got to have their regular reunions, and the warmth of shared memories and experience, those who worked either in codebreaking or in the 'Y' Service were denied this. When they left the Park, it was as though they had never been there. A few might have known each

OPPOSITE The annual
reunions have been a source
of great pleasure and pride
to veterans.

RIGHT Together for Radio
4's *The Reunion* – from left:
John Herivel, the Hon Sarah
Baring, Mavis Batey, host Sue
MacGregor, Lord Briggs and
Ruth Bourne.

other socially but for the majority, their war years were consigned to the shadows, with few chances ever to meet up with peers, still less to finally openly discuss the work that they did. During the

the police, it was Turing himself who was prosecuted, for 'gross indecency'. Professor Max Newman and Hugh Alexander stood by him as he received that sentence of chemical castration, and

R.K. Enterprises (London) Ltd.
Ron King presents at the
WILTON HALL, Bletchley
THIS SATURDAY, 13th JANUARY
8 - 11.30 p.m.   Admission 8/6
Britain's No. 1 Recording Star
ADAM FAITH

SATURDAY, 20th JANUARY
THE KARL DENVER TRIO

SATURDAY, 27th JANUARY
THE JOHN BARRY SEVEN

FEBRUARY 3rd
Closed owing to previous bookings

FEBRUARY 10th
Reopen with the dynamic
VINCE EAGER

Ron King presents at the
WILTON HALL, BLETCHLEY
THIS SATURDAY, 14th MARCH
GENE VINCENT
Plus THE MUSTANGS
8 - 11.30 p.m.   Admission 6/6

MARCH 21st
NEIL CHRISTIAN & The Crusaders

MARCH 28th
THE ROLLING STONES
8 - 11.30 p.m.   Admission 10/-
Tickets can be obtained at the hall on Wednesday
and Saturday evenings only or at the door on the night
Doors will be open at 7 p.m.

APRIL 4th
JOHNNY KIDD and The Pirates
All Rights of Admission Reserved

TOP TWENTY CLUB
OPEN EVERY WEDNESDAY
8 - 11 p.m.   Admission 2/6

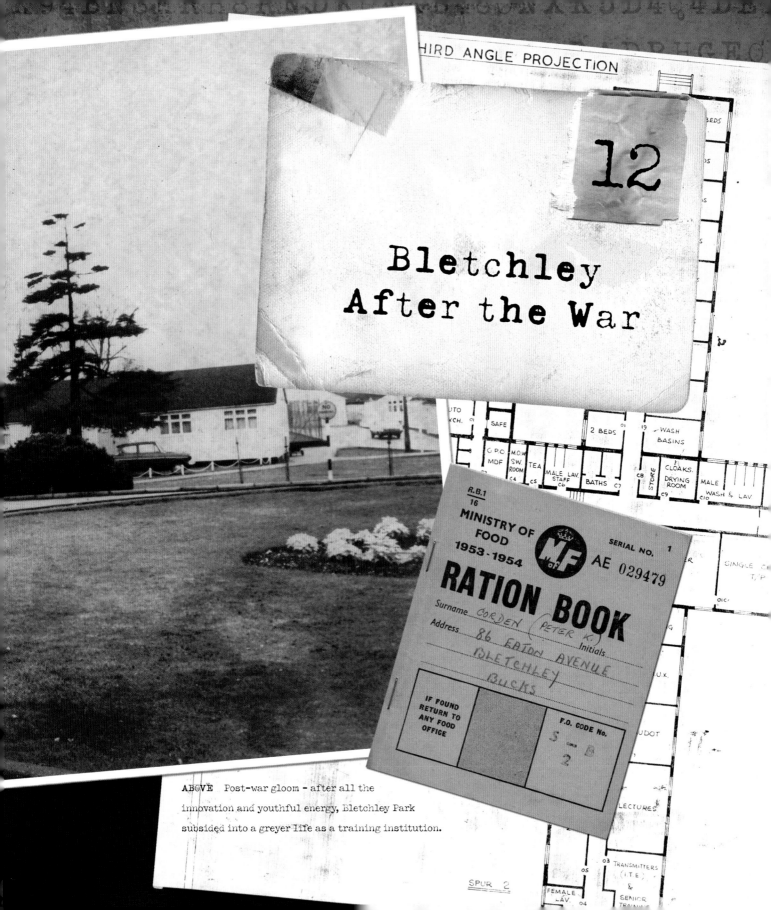

12

Bletchley
After the War

MINISTRY OF FOOD
1953-1954
R.B.1
16
SERIAL NO. 1
AE 029479

RATION BOOK

Surname CORDEN (PETER K.)
Initials.
Address 86 EATON AVENUE
BLETCHLEY
BUCKS

IF FOUND RETURN TO ANY FOOD OFFICE

F.O. CODE No.
S — B
2

ABOVE Post-war gloom – after all the innovation and youthful energy, Bletchley Park subsided into a greyer life as a training institution.

THIS PAGE The architecture and the red telephone box clearly marked Bletchley out as an archetypally English boffin establishment. But its war-time life was completely secret until the 1970s.

THE DEMANDS OF PEACETIME WERE DIFFERENT, BUT NO LESS INTENSE IN THEIR OWN WAY. THE BRITISH GOVERNMENT STILL NEEDED AN ESTABLISHMENT THAT – AS IN THE PRE-WAR YEARS – WOULD ASSIDUOUSLY LISTEN TO AND MONITOR AND DECODE SIGNALS FROM ALL AROUND THE WORLD. THE OPENING STAGES OF THE COLD WAR WERE ONLY ONE ELEMENT IN THIS: BRITAIN STILL HAD AN EMPIRE, AND OUTPOSTS, AND GLOBAL INTERESTS. IN TERMS OF A FULL-TIME CODEBREAKING OPERATION, THOUGH, IT WAS TIME TO VACATE BLETCHLEY PARK. COMMANDER EDWARD TRAVIS, WHO WAS TO STAY ON AS THE DIRECTOR, NOW FELT THAT IT WAS TIME TO MOVE BACK TO THE CAPITAL.

Things had rather moved on since the days when the Government Code and Cypher School was based in St James's Park; the bulky new technology meant that such a constrained inner London setting would not be suitable. Because Russia had yet to develop the nuclear bomb – that would follow several years later – the idea of a nuclear strike on the capital was not at that stage a consideration. Nonetheless, there were other good security reasons for staying out of the centre of London, a measure of invisibility being one of them. And there were sites on the fringes of the city out of which bombe machines had been working throughout the latter stages of the War. There was Stanmore in the northwest and – several miles west of that – a large station in Eastcote, Middlesex. It was neatly positioned on the Piccadilly Line, for swift access to the centre of town, but the site itself was anonymous and leafy and suburban, and drew no attention to itself at all.

By April 1946, the wartime clear-out of the Bletchley site was pretty much complete. Every corner, every cranny, had been scoured for sensitive material: dropped decrypts, tiny machine components, all down to the last scrap of paper. The estate would swiftly fill up again, as we shall see below, partly with a GCHQ offshoot, but also with a variety of other functions and institutions. But some of the staff – among whom was young Mimi Galilee – decided to make the transfer. From the start, the Eastcote base itself was a slightly lowering prospect. The utilitarian concrete buildings that housed the bombes were held to be in 'poor condition' and 'very cramped'. However, there was a new generation of recruits coming in; a fresh batch of mathematicians to blend in with some of the old Bletchley hands. And some of the atmosphere of the old establishment persisted in the six years or so that the newly minted GCHQ stayed at Eastcote, before its more permanent move to Cheltenham. There were chess societies, plus fondly remembered tennis and cricket matches. One veteran recalled how Hugh Alexander – while an undisputed genius both at chess and codebreaking – was less impressive near the stumps.

The workload also remained impressively heavy; this was the time of a continued (and in peacetime unprecedented) signals/intelligence understanding between Britain and America – the UK–USA alliance. Because Britain's territories – the Empire and the Commonwealth – were still so extraordinarily extensive, the Americans were in a few cases rather reliant on these far-flung outposts for crucial intercepts and intelligence. The British Empire would dissolve with remarkable speed over the course of the next twenty years but until then, the fledgling GCHQ already had a mighty burden to shoulder. In the early 1950s, the size of the operation – plus the new threat of nuclear strike from a Soviet Union that had started testing its own weapons – necessitated a further move. This was to a location that in some ways would prove to be the true spiritual successor to that 55-acre Buckinghamshire estate. Under the guise of roving civil servants on the look-out for new office space, GCHQ operatives scouted out various candidates outside London; at one point, even Canada was mooted as a potential base. But soon they found what they were looking for: a smart county town which by coincidence had a collection of government offices that were being wound down. The site had space and – crucially – capacity for a great number of telephone landlines. The proposal was put to a frankly delighted Cheltenham town council (which had been anxious about the offices closing down). Now the town of Cheltenham would have an entirely new community descending upon it, engaged upon work every bit as highly confidential and sensitive as that conducted at Bletchley. And as well as Hugh Alexander, there were other veterans such as Arthur Bonsall (later

to rise to great prominence) and GCHQ's new Director, Sir Eric Jones.

GCHQ kept one prominent link with the old Bletchley Park site: this is where its Central Training School was now based. But the old huts and the house also played host to some other concerns. The General Post Office also used the estate as a training centre – this, broadly, for telecommunications operatives, working on high-frequency transmitters and receivers. Again, though, technology swiftly began to outstrip these: satellites would become the next big thing. There was also an unexpected technological upset there: namely, the electrification of the West Coast railway line in the early 1970s, which apparently interfered with the radio masts on the site. Rubbing alongside all of this, though, was a teacher training college for women (which arrived in 1948), then later a hostel and even a magistrates' court. By the late 1960s, the area had a fresh centre of gravity, in the form of the new town of Milton Keynes – an

BELOW Bletchley Park's activities were moved to the London suburb of Eastcote – the base is seen from above. This area has been cleared to make way for luxury flats.

LEFT The huts and the blocks were left echoing and empty, and all the technology was stripped out. Some was sent on to Eastcote in Middlesex – and some of the Bletchley staff went with it.

urban development that swallowed some of the old local villages. It was (and is) just four miles from Bletchley. In the mid-1980s, when the GPO was privatised by Mrs Thatcher's government and transformed into British Telecom, the company stayed on the site for training purposes for several more years. On top of this, the Civil Aviation Authority also had space there at this time. It must have been a puzzling and rather louring prospect though: a few of the old wartime huts had been demolished, but some – plus the great featureless concrete blocks – remained. Some of them had even been renovated to an extent, in order to form study bedrooms for the training centre. Thus various different branches of organisations added their own frankly unlovely 1970s contribution: anonymous square slabs of glass and concrete. There was no clue as to the estate's wonderful – and colourful – wartime life, at least until the mid-1970s, when the silence began to lift. Even after this, in the 1980s, it must have been tricky to associate this drab and anonymous estate with the inspiration and ingenuity it had housed just a few years previously. And the house itself was slowly beginning to disintegrate.

In 1976, the teacher training college left the estate. Eleven years later, in 1987, so too did the training arm of GCHQ. In 1993, British Telecom packed up its operations there, as did the Civil Aviation Authority branch. There came a perilous point where the house was facing a similarly bleak prospect to the one presented some fifty-five years earlier when Sir George Leon sold up: it could quite easily have been demolished, as indeed could the huts and blocks. If it had not been for the determination of a few passionate individuals, the physical legacy of Bletchley Park might have been lost for ever.

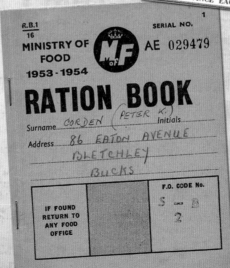

ABOVE Wilton Hall had been constructed for the codebreakers – but it later found new life as a venue for acts like The Rolling Stones and The John Barry Seven.

LEFT Ration books were still in use well into the early 1950s. Veterans recalled the grimness of that post-war austerity – by contrast, the Bletchley canteen seemed a cornucopia.

BELOW Loon pants and mini-skirts aside, Bletchley Park at least
continued the tradition of young people gathered together in one
institution – now used for telecoms training – and making full
use of the ballroom.

OPPOSITE Considering the extemporisation of Bletchley's early
days, its later organisation was meticulous and technocratic.

SOCIAL AND WELFARE

This is the seco
its importance lyi
headed by a Welf
background of we
comfort, with the
people of both sex

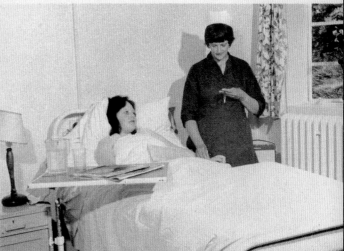

*The well-equipped Sick Bay is staffed by a qualified Sister and nursing staff.
There are morning and evening surgeries and the Sick Bay has adequate
facilities for in-patient nursing. The Centre also has its own local medical
adviser. The service is further supplemented by experienced First Aid personnel
who are members of the staff at both Bletchley Park and Drayton Parslow.*

*The residential acc
comfort, but also f
so that the studen
The Centre has a
from popular mag
related to the Pos
are on open shelv*

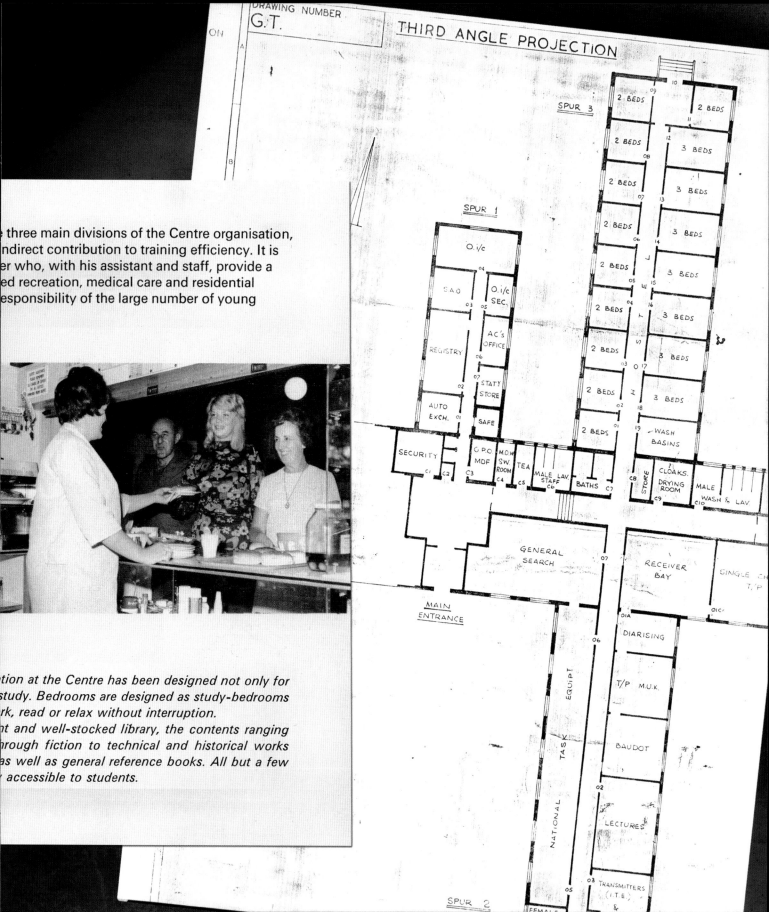

DRAWING NUMBER

G.T.

ON

THIRD ANGLE PROJECTION

...e three main divisions of the Centre organisation,
...ndirect contribution to training efficiency. It is
...er who, with his assistant and staff, provide a
...ed recreation, medical care and residential
...esponsibility of the large number of young

...tion at the Centre has been designed not only for
...study. Bedrooms are designed as study-bedrooms
...rk, read or relax without interruption.
...nt and well-stocked library, the contents ranging
...hrough fiction to technical and historical works
...as well as general reference books. All but a few
...r accessible to students.

SPUR 3

SPUR 1

2 BEDS · 2 BEDS
2 BEDS · 3 BEDS
2 BEDS · 3 BEDS
2 BEDS · 3 BEDS
2 BEDS · 3 BEDS
2 BEDS · 3 BEDS
2 BEDS · 3 BEDS
2 BEDS · 3 BEDS
2 BEDS · WASH BASINS

O.i/c
SAO · O.i/c SEC.
AC's OFFICE
REGISTRY
STAT'Y STORE
AUTO EXCH. · SAFE

SECURITY
G.P.O. MDF · M.O.W. SW. ROOM · TEA · MALE LAV. STAFF · BATHS · STORE · CLOAKS. DRYING ROOM · MALE WASH & LAV.

GENERAL SEARCH · RECEIVER BAY · SINGLE CH... T/P

MAIN ENTRANCE · DIARISING

T/P M.U.K.

NATIONAL TASK EQUIP'T · BAUDOT

LECTURES

TRANSMITTERS (I.T.E.)

SPUR 2

RIGHT Before the Bletchley Park Trust was formed, many of the huts and blocks had fallen into a state of advanced and creeping dilapidation.

Rescue and Renovation

B ARELY ONE HUNDRED YEARS AFTER IT WAS BUILT, BLETCHLEY PARK – BY THE EARLY 1990S – WAS FACING THE PROSPECT OF BEING TURNED INTO A VAST SUPERMARKET AND A NEW HOUSING DEVELOPMENT. IT WAS EMPTY AND DISUSED. THE HUTS WERE ROTTING; AND BECAUSE OF LEAKS IN THE ROOF, THE MAIN HOUSE WAS SIMILARLY FALLING APART. IT PRESENTED A MELANCHOLIC SPECTACLE. IN 1991, THE LOCAL BLETCHLEY HISTORICAL AND ARCHAEOLOGICAL ASSOCIATION WAS CONVINCED THAT THOSE WHO HAD WORKED THERE WOULD NEVER AGAIN HAVE A CHANCE TO SEE IT; AND SO THE SOCIETY SET ABOUT TRACKING DOWN AS MANY BLETCHLEY PARK VETERANS AS IT COULD.

The idea was that the veterans would be invited to a grand farewell party. Most of them would not have seen the site since the War. Thanks to some assiduous research, not to mention the putting out of many feelers, the society managed to muster an impressive 400 veterans for the occasion. The event turned out to be terrifically moving and – for those on the committee of the society – fantastically eye-opening. Suddenly the continued neglect of this historic location felt absurd and also – given the scale of the Park's achievements – outrageous.

And it was at this point that these Bletchley enthusiasts seriously set to work on preserving the Park as best they could. The tactics were laudably clever. One local councillor in Milton Keynes had noted, for instance, that the great avenues of old trees planted in the era of the Leons, and before, were as much under threat as any of the buildings; and he saw to it in 1992 that a conservation order was slapped on them. This had the knock-on effect of safeguarding a substantial proportion of the Park. That same year, the Bletchley Park Trust was formed. The estate and its lands were tangled up in a labyrinth of ownership, between British Telecom and the aviation arm of the Civil Service. And it was with these bodies that the Trust sailed into immediate negotiations. Time was against them; for instance, in the main house the

ABOVE The Bletchley Park Trust raised awareness that these buildings had great historical significance, and should be preserved for future generations.

OPPOSITE The film *Enigma* (2001), starring Dougray Scott and Kate Winslet, and based on the Robert Harris novel, helped attract publicity for the Park and its museum, even though the story's Polish villain went down badly with some.

ballroom, with its ornate plaster ceiling of 'drooping bosoms' as Sarah Baring had so poetically put it, was in grave danger of collapse. If they did not act fast, then there would be precious little legacy to preserve at all.

HRH the Duke of Kent became the Trust's chief patron and in 1994 the site was tentatively opened to the public as a sparse – but deeply atmospheric – museum. To begin with, this was a very limited operation, with the Park opened up once every other weekend. But the story of Bletchley was now at last starting to become more widely known. In 1995, a novel by journalist-turned-author Robert Harris became a bestseller: *Enigma*. It was a fictionalised thriller set in and around the Park – rich in atmospheric description, and true to the enormous tensions and anxieties that the work had produced. This romanticised account

ABOVE Even the sturdier blocks – the buildings that had once housed the most secret technology in Europe – were not immune to neglect and entropy.

LEFT Rebuilding and repair work involved years of hard work and assiduous fund-raising.

of the codebreakers' work could only have been a help and it was around this time that the museum began operating more regular opening hours. There was also the publication of *Code Breakers* – a collection of essays from a range of veterans, pulled together by Harry Hinsley and Alan Stripp, which laid out in full detail, complete with wiring diagrams, how those miracles of decryption had been achieved. On top of this was a steady increase in press interest, particularly on those occasions when codebreaking veterans made their first returns to the Park since the War. The significance of the estate was gaining wider recognition. By the end of the decade, the Bletchley Park Trust had secured a valuable concession: a 250-year leasehold on the most historic areas of the Park.

Then there were the films – one a tremendous hit, the other a source of wild exasperation. Michael Apted's 2001 screen version of *Enigma*, starring Dougray Scott and Kate Winslet, was not filmed at the Park itself – instead, the location was the very much grander and prettier Chicheley Hall, also in Buckinghamshire (which had actually seen service during the War as a base for the Special Operations Executive). Nonetheless, the success of the film generated an enormous amount of interest in the real Park. At the time of its release, Oliver and Sheila Lawn were interviewed by the press and asked – continually – if they were the couple on whom the romantic leads in the film were based. They played along with the brouhaha with great good humour. The other film, one that still evokes sharp in-breaths of

irritation, was *U-571* (2000). This told the story of how an Enigma machine was captured from a German submarine in 1942 by the Americans, and how it was entirely thanks to them that the codes were cracked. In the end titles, there was an acknowledgement to the British sailors of HMS *Bulldog*, who had carried out the real operation against *U-110* in 1941, some months before the US entered the War. Prime Minister Tony Blair agreed with a questioner in the House of Commons who declared it an 'affront'. Yet this seething controversy had the upside of focusing attention upon the real heroes of the Enigma story.

The strangest episode during this period was when, in 2000, a four-rotor Abwehr Enigma machine was stolen from the Park, despite security; some time after, the Park received ransom notes, demanding extortionate sums for its return or it would be destroyed. Then, in a bizarre twist, the machine was posted to the BBC office of the presenter Jeremy Paxman. Odd though the story

RIGHT Broadcaster Jeremy Paxman, himself the centre of an enigma, when a stolen machine was sent in a parcel to his Newsnight office.

ABOVE The sorry state of Hut 3 in the early 1990s – yet in another sense, it was remarkable that such makeshift, temporary structures were still standing.

LEFT The late Tony Sale – a computer expert whose meticulous recreation of the Colossus machine was a stupendous feat, and a huge Bletchley attraction.

BELOW AND OPPOSITE BELOW The once-grand cricket pavilion was under threat of demolition for years. The decay on some parts of the estate – and in the main house – was heartbreaking to see.

was, it alerted a wider public to the idea of guided tours around the Park. And the return of the machine also highlighted how the Park was working to safeguard this still mysterious heritage. Secret history was now being bathed in the gaudiest limelight, and deservedly so.

By 2004, the museum was thriving (even if the Park's finances were not), with an array of fascinating displays, and it was opening every day. What also gave it tremendous appeal to visitors was the

small army of dedicated volunteers who kept the place running – not least of which were the veterans who gave superb informed tours. Former Wrens Ruth Bourne and Jean Valentine were not merely experts, but also captivating public speakers. Word spread further and more and more special visiting parties came in. Added to this were enthusiasts such as the computer expert Tony Sale. His epic reconstruction of the Colossus machine – the original blueprints of which had, as we have seen, been consigned to the

flames – stands as a monument both to his acute ingenuity but also to his dedication. For a younger generation that takes iPads for granted, to gaze now upon this recreation is to understand the painstaking and often mad brilliance of those taking the first steps in computing. Very few of them would be able to operate it with any confidence that they were doing it right. The same might be true of the bombe reconstructions: in broad terms, that was the era when technology first leaped ahead of its operators, the workings and functions of these new machines many times more esoteric than even the most advanced radio set. These Bletchley attractions – the re-builds, plus the original Enigma machines, plus the refreshingly un-dumbed-down displays – started to attract ever greater numbers of visitors. The Park Trust also found another valuable revenue stream: that of letting out serviced office accommodation within the estate. It could also be used for business and

ABOVE The house and its grounds have been restored to a proud state that Sir Herbert and Lady Fanny Leon might have recognised. Taken from the exact same view as on page 22.

commercial conferences, as none of these activities would impinge on the Park's historical areas in any way. Yet still the future was far from secure and, despite the milling visitors, the house and the huts still needed a huge amount of work. In the case of the huts, a couple of these buildings had tarpaulins for roofs. These structures had only been built to last five or six years – no one during the War would have anticipated that anyone would have wanted to see them fifty or sixty years afterwards.

In 2008 there came, at last, the sense that the importance of the site was being recognised in more official circles: English Heritage gave £330,000 for the much-needed repair of the house's roof. By now, the Park's annual reunions for veterans, held every September, were not merely a part of the local calendar, but an event to which visitors came from all over the country. There was – and still is – something ineffably moving about seeing the once silent, once invisible codebreakers and Wrens lining up proudly in front of the house for the group photograph after the service of remembrance.

The rescue of the house and huts and blocks, which looked in the early 1990s beyond the realms of possibility, had found – nearly – a firm footing, a grounded stability. All of that was made possible not merely by the initial committee, but also by the terrific enthusiasm of volunteers and veterans alike. Their work combined to pull off the most remarkable of all feats: it recreated, unselfconsciously, the slightly anarchic, extemporised feel of the

wartime establishment. It wasn't just the look of the place that had been preserved, it was the feel and the ethos of it too. The visitors wandering around had no difficulty at all in picturing distracted codebreakers throwing cups into lakes, or in the huts hunched over columns of five-letter groups, or in the house, being ushered through to sign the Official Secrets Act. The spirit had remained.

OPPOSITE BELOW and BELOW The breathtakingly researched Bletchley Park reconstructions of Hut 8 and the Directorate – down to cardigans over chairs – in the main house also feature immersive sound effects that capture the atmosphere of the time.

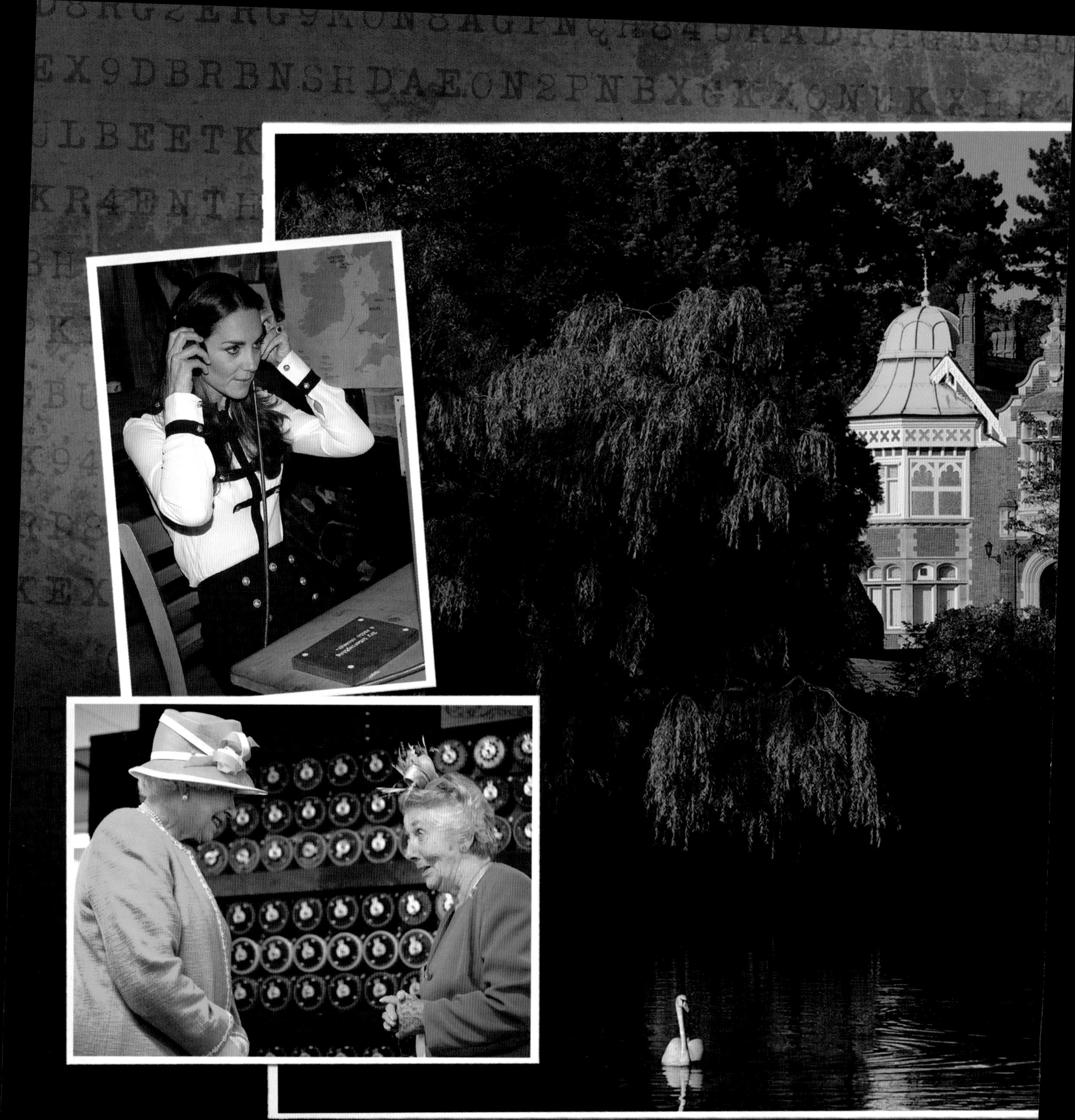

Royals, Dignitaries - and James Bond

LEFT The renovated Bletchley Park now attracts around 200,000 visitors a year, and further improvements are in progress.

Money is one thing – but that alone does not breathe fresh life into institutions. So while the Park's success in securing the help of the Heritage Lottery Fund is terrific (and a tribute to the ceaseless work of Dr Sue Black and Simon Greenish MBE, among many others) we must also acknowledge how the increasing interest of the great and the good has been helping the Park too. The presence of celebrities never hurts; and broadcaster and writer Stephen Fry has been continually vocal in his support. He has visited the Park a few times and never wastes an opportunity to publicise it, either on his television shows or in among his thousands of tweets. Nor should any other show-business support be viewed in snobbish terms: whatever generates interest in the Park is also helping to preserve it.

One of the more agreeable problems the Park now faces is that huge numbers of film and television crews are besieging it on an almost daily basis. There are the frequent occasions when news stories break – wartime racing pigeons carrying codes, for instance – to thrust Bletchley back into the spotlight. Take the recent story, unearthed by Michael Smith, that Agatha Christie was investigated by MI5 during the War because of her espionage/detective novel *N or M?*, which featured a character called Major Bletchley. Christie happened to be friends with Dilly Knox; MI5 wanted to know if she was trying to tip a sinister wink to enemy powers. The answer, of course, was no, not even remotely. It was simply a coincidence. Yet such tales tend to bring the world's cameras to the Park, and they have to be fitted in around all the visitors.

Interest goes beyond the news. A few years back, the popular BBC Sunday night staple *Antiques Roadshow* filmed two editions in the grounds of the house. This made a perfect fit alongside other recent huge attractions to the estate: vintage car shows and 1940s family festivals, featuring dances and music from the period. (There were also notable unexpected treasure stories on *Antiques Roadshow*, including a glass vase that had been bought for

ABOVE Bletchley Park supporter Stephen Fry is fascinated by Tony Sale's intricate rebuild of the Colossus machine.

OPPOSITE Her Majesty the Queen meets veteran codebreakers Oliver and Sheila Lawn on a visit in 2011. In her speech, she gave 'heartfelt thanks' to all Bletchley's recruits 'on behalf of a grateful nation'.

£1 was valued at £36,000.) This is to say nothing of a cavalcade of documentaries either about Bletchley directly or about the people who worked there. For a house that twice faced demolition, it is now becoming as recognisable to a wider public as Highclere Castle or Strawberry Hill.

In 2009, when it was decided that Bletchley Park veterans should each receive a commemorative medal for the work that they did there, the cause was taken up eagerly by the then Labour Foreign Secretary David Miliband, who spent hours at the Park, chatting to veterans and to members of the Trust. One veteran recalls that – even though she has been a life-long Tory voter – Mr Miliband had such good manners and such a lively interest in the Park and all who had been there that she declared she would have happily voted for him. His Tory successor at the Foreign Office, William Hague, has also visited the Park. Elsewhere, in 2009, Prime Minister Gordon Brown issued a posthumous apology to Alan Turing for the appalling treatment he had received after the War. In welcoming this, the Bletchley Park Trust hammered home the point that, in helping to preserve the Park, the importance of Alan Turing's achievements would receive their rightful celebration.

There have been pleasantly unexpected bursts of publicity from the glitzier end of show business too; such as the occasion, in 2012, when the television reality show *MasterChef* broadcast a special celebrity edition from Bletchley Park. The celebrities, including Emma Kennedy, rather appropriately had to prepare dishes for judges such as Sir Arthur Bonsall, veteran codebreaker

ABOVE When the popular BBC TV series *Antiques Roadshow* filmed editions at Bletchley, it helped bring more visitors to the museum. The Park stages many special events, from vintage car rallies to TV specials.

RIGHT 007 actor Sir Roger Moore on a visit to the Park in 2008, bringing with him an array of James Bond's favourite cars.

and also a former Director of GCHQ. Throughout, the veterans were invited to compare the complicated dishes with the fare that they had enjoyed – or emphatically not enjoyed – in the Park's wartime canteen.

Another entertaining guest visit came from Sir Roger Moore, the former James Bond actor. There were several pleasing echoes here: 007's creator, Ian Fleming, had himself been in Naval Intelligence during the War, and as such had frequent dealings with Bletchley Park and the codebreaking operation. But while Fleming had the necessary security clearance to visit, it is unlikely that his fictional creation Bond would have been granted it. The

Park's work was very strictly 'need to know' and the vast majority of agents were not let in on it. Sir Roger himself revelled in his visit, and got to meet veterans such as Mavis and Keith Batey. It is a measure of the power of the Bletchley story that even a film star cannot grab all the limelight here. Nor indeed would he have wanted to.

It is no exaggeration, though, to say that one special visit that has meant everything to surviving veterans was that paid by Her Majesty the Queen in 2012. The event was kept every bit as close a secret as the original code-work itself; veterans who were tipped the wink in advance, in order to get ready, admirably proved once more their ability not to say a word to a soul. The Queen arrived with the Duke of Edinburgh and, despite the numbers of proud veterans lined up to meet them, there was still time for spirited exchanges. One veteran recalls how the Queen showed great interest in how the wartime work remained confidential – and in the unspoken assumption of duty that went with that. The Queen and Prince Philip were also given the expert guided tour to the bombe and Colossus reconstructions. It is always startling to remember that Queen Elizabeth – then

BELOW Veterans and their families gather together in the courtyard on the day of the Royal visit – the first time Her Majesty had been there.

BELOW STANDING Codebreaking veteran Sir Arthur Bonsall, standing before the impressive Bletchley memorial designed by Charles Gurrey, unveiled by Her Majesty the Queen in 2011.

BELOW SEATED Veterans Sheila and Oliver Lawn – who have often been asked by newspapers and TV organisations for help with unsolved codes, ancient and modern.

ABOVE HRH Princess Elizabeth hard at work as an ATS volunteer during the War at around the time that the Tunny codes were being broken.

LEFT During the course of their tour, the Queen and the Duke of Edinburgh met veteran Jean Valentine and codebreaker Jerry Roberts MBE (**BOTTOM LEFT**).

ABOVE Veteran Ruth Bourne was on hand to guide the Queen and the Duke of Edinburgh through the fiendish complexities of the Enigma

Princess Elizabeth – was an ATS girl, a truck mechanic, when this technology was coming into play. Possibly another reason why her visit had such an enormous impact upon Bletchley veterans was that they recognised that she too was a veteran – albeit from another side of the war effort. The wider point is that the visit bestowed an even greater sense that the Bletchley Park estate is now an ineradicable feature of the historical landscape; almost the equivalent of a Royal Warrant. Nor has interest from the royal family diminished at all. Not long ago, the Prince of Wales hosted a charitable fund-raising dinner at St James's Palace, at which veteran Jean Valentine spoke; so entertaining was she that the Prince

was seen wiping tears of laughter away. Even more recently, the Duchess of Cornwall has visited the Park, as part of an effort to raise recognition of the pivotal role of women throughout the war.

There has also been a terrific amount of interest – and indeed support – from the American internet search engine giant Google. It was with their help that Bletchley Park was able to acquire and

BELOW The Duchess of Cornwall looks at an Enigma Machine alongside code breaker Eileen Johnson.

ABOVE Codebreakers Keith and Mavis Batey prepare to demonstrate Enigma for HRH The Prince of Wales and the Duchess of Cornwall.

RIGHT Prince Charles unveils a commemorative tablet.

In commemoration of the visit of
Their Royal Highnesses
The Prince of Wales
and
The Duchess of Cornwall
to Bletchley Park on 24th July 2008

ANOTHER ROYAL VISIT

HRH THE DUCHESS OF CAMBRIDGE'S VISIT TO THE PARK IN 2014 WAS DOUBLY MOVING; FIRST, BECAUSE
THAT DAY SHE LEARNED SO MUCH ABOUT THE SECRET WORK THAT HER GRANDMOTHER VALERIE
GLASSBARROW DID THERE – AN EXTRAORDINARY COINCIDENCE BROUGHT TO LIGHT BY THE BLETCHLEY
PARK TRUST. SECONDLY, BECAUSE THE DUCHESS GOT THE CHANCE TO MEET DELIGHTED VETERANS, AND
TO HEAR THEIR WONDERFUL STORIES. VALERIE GLASSBARROW, AS IT HAPPENED, HAD BEEN INVOLVED IN
AN ESPECIALLY PATIENCE-TRYING ASPECT OF THE OPERATION, INVOLVING MONITORING OUTPUT FROM 'Y'
STATIONS. HER VISIT GAVE THE DUCHESS THE PROUD KNOWLEDGE THAT ONE OF HER FOREBEARS WAS
SO CLOSE TO THE NERVE CENTRE OF THE WAR – ADDED TO AN RAF PILOT GRANDFATHER, PETER MIDDLETON,
WHO SHOT DOWN V-I MISSILES.

save Alan Turing's papers; they are now on display in the Park's museum. With Google has come a range of VIP visits, some still top secret: a guest on one occasion was an American actor who – it is fair to say – has one of the most recognisable voices in the entire world. Unfortunately, the Bletchley Park Trust's own official secrets act forbids me from saying anything more! Elsewhere, Google has taken a close interest in the work of Dr Tommy Flowers and recently produced a film paying tribute to his role in kicking off what we might term the Google age. Naturally the executives of other global computing concerns – Microsoft and Apple – have also taken an assiduous interest in the Park and the museum. It is said that in Silicon Valley, an entire young generation of software

specialists revere Alan Turing and Max Newman as the colossi of their field.

The arrangement with Google has also helped to cement further Bletchley's financial future. So while on the one hand the royal visits and the endorsements from cabinet ministers and other dignitaries have undoubteldy enshrined the Park's status as part of the historical establishment, this interest from global giants is an indicator of the debt they feel they owe to the breakthroughs that were made here. It is impossible to think of any other institution in the world that can count both Her Majesty the Queen and Californian computer whizz-kids as ardent admirers.

BELOW A perennially popular event at Bletchley Park is its special 1940s day – featuring vintage clothes, memorabilia, and terrific music.

Bletchley Park
Season Ticket
a year to discover
more secrets.

Enjoy your visits

LEFT & BELOW Loving attention to detail is a key feature of Bletchley Park – even down to the beautifully designed museum season tickets.

SCRAMBLE!
Don't come and tell
Ring like 'ELL.

Over recent months, spectacular restoration work has proceeded apace at the Park; not merely the atmospheric rebuild of Hut 8 and Alan Turing's office, but also key rooms in the main house, dressed authentically – down to cardigans on the backs of chairs and cigarette butts in ashtrays – to give visitors an exact flavour of Bletchley in the War. There are sound effects too, such as the engine noise of a motorcycle dispatch rider outside the huts, conveying vividly the busy, urgent air. On top of this, there has been the lively addition of interactive computer exhibits – allowing younger visitors to try out the complexity of cipher-breaking and wartime technology – plus also special exhibitions, such as that devoted to the World War One efforts of Room 40. The extent to which the story of the codebreakers has beguiled the national imagination is also evident in the way that their work now materialises so frequently in popular culture. In 2012, Anna Maxwell-Martin and Rachael Stirling headed an impressive cast for an ITV detective thriller series, *The Bletchley Circle*. Set in the 1950s, when the vow of silence lay at its heaviest, the series involved four fictional women, linked by their time at Bletchley, who join forces against a serial killer when they begin to see the patterns in his frightful crimes. It ran to a second series, involving the four friends getting caught up in further espionage adventures, and proved particularly popular in America; which in turn generated a lot of transatlantic tourist interest in Bletchley Park itself.

Then in late 2014 came a critically acclaimed film loosely based upon Andrew Hodge's biography of

LEFT The Olympic torch, carried by Hazel Staten, came to Bletchley in 2012, bringing with it an echo of Turing's talent for (amateur) long-distance running. In 1947, he ran a marathon in 2 hours and 46 minutes, which would have been an extremely respectable Olympic time.

Alan Turing. *The Imitation Game*, starring Benedict Cumberbatch and Keira Knightley, which won an Oscar for its screenplay by Graham Moore, was a box-office success on both sides of the Atlantic. The film might have made a few dramatic adjustments to history, as some critics and writers cheerfully pointed out (among which was making Alistair Denniston a gruff and vinegary enemy of Turing; making Joan Clarke a woman who had wandered in off the street to take part in a crossword competition as opposed to a fiercely skilled mathematician in her own right; and implying that there was only one bombe machine, operated by Turing himself). But as one wise Bletchley veteran laughed: 'It's only a film'. And the wider point was that again, it inspired fresh swathes of visitors to come to Bletchley. They were able to match the drama to the reality themselves. Added to this, Benedict Cumberbatch's sensitive and intelligent portrayal of Turing further helped to seal the real man into the national consciousness.

In the name of research, Cumberbatch visited the Park a couple of times, where he learned a great deal, including some of the abstruse mathematical beauty of the codebreakers' successes.

As with *Enigma* (2001) – the film based on Robert Harris's thriller – the location work for *The Imitation Game* actually took place at properties all over Buckinghamshire and Oxfordshire. But important bar-room scenes – are there any other kind? – were filmed at BP, fittingly, in the ballroom of the main house. This then became the centrepiece of an exhibition revolving around the film. The actors said that they found it very easy to imagine the ghosts of Bletchley recruits still having a presence there. In an interview with Bletchley Park, Cumberbatch said: 'To work where these people breathed, lived, loved, worked, struggled, kept secrets, were quietly, stoically heroic, was overwhelming. It's incredibly important that it's open to the public, and that it is something that is well-funded and supported and continues, because this is our history.'

Cumberbatch's star power may have brought thousands flocking to see the real site; but Bletchley is also now, rather brilliantly, cropping up in popular culture everywhere, from *Doctor Who* plays to mentions by the Guardian columnist Marina Hyde. In her witty 'Lost In Showbiz' column, she takes the often impenetrably daft utterances of pop stars and celebrities, and claims to have them sent them 'to Bletchley Park' in the hope that some sense can be brought to bear. At the other end of the scale, in terms of high culture, the classical composer Nico Muhly recently visited Bletchley Park with counter-tenor Iestyn Davies; both men learning more about Alan Turing's War – and his theories involving 'thinking machines' and the nature of human consciousness – before performing Muhly's haunting new operatic work based on Turing's life, called *Sentences*, at the Barbican in London. The larger more important point is that thanks to the unstinting work of the Bletchley Park Trust, the extraordinary achievements of all those who worked here are now guaranteed to echo down the generations, in every shape and form, and on a site dedicated to celebrating every aspect and every level of the operation.

This is all having said nothing of Bletchley's visitors, who are arriving in ever greater numbers year by year. It is estimated currently that nearly 200,000 people go through those Park gates annually. To this end, the Park made some dramatic changes to accommodate these growing numbers; as well as the streamlined lay-out of the block exhibitions, the huts and blocks themselves

LEFT A critical hit for ITV (and a cult favourite in America too), the thriller series *The Bletchley Circle* was set in the 1950s and starred Anna Maxwell-Martin, Rachael Stirling, Sophie Rundle and Julie Graham as a group of friends who worked at Bletchley Park during the War. The producers described the pressing need to get even the tiniest set details absolutely right.

RIGHT The premise of *The Bletchley Circle* – that a group of women get to employ their secret skills in detective work after the War – might have had an element of wish-fulfilment. For many in real life, the post-war years brought the culture shock of purely domestic routines.

BELOW *The Bletchley Circle* also portrayed the stresses that life at Bletchley had brought; skill and experience were hard won.

were extensively renovated. There is still so much to exhibit, so much for the visitor to see. The result of this is that – by contrast with the ghostly, quiet, abandoned site of twenty years ago – Bletchley on a daily basis now teems with as many people as it did during those war years. As well as the painstaking hut reconstructions, and the work carried out upon the interior of the house (which architectural historians are now beginning to look upon a little more fondly), there are ever more tours, conducted by ever more volunteers, who have been given the most stringent training; almost as stringent as that received by the Wrens being sent to operate the Colossus machines.

The Park is teeming with life; and while the lifeline of the Lottery Heritage Fund might mean that some aspects of it seem to become a little sleeker and better organised, this too is in keeping with the way that the working methods of the Park changed mid-war – from the genteel chaos of Alastair Denniston to the well-oiled routines of his deputy, Commander Travis.

This emergence from the darkness, this belated celebration, commemorated with a special statue near the entrance to the Park, has been terrifically important to the

LEFT Benedict Cumberbatch as Alan Turing. In an interview, Oscar-nominated Cumberbatch said of Turing: 'He was an incredibly sensitive human being in a very brutal world.'

surviving veterans. Over the last twenty years, the regeneration of Bletchley Park finally gave them a focal point for memories, and a chance to reunite; those simple things denied them all those previous decades ago. For the annual reunion weekends, veterans travel from all over the country, and revel in the special talks and events and meals. The melancholy and inescapable fact is that numbers are dwindling year by year. But thanks to the Bletchley Park Trust, the estate has grown into something far greater than a shrine or a monument: the fascinating museum and displays – and still-growing archive – are there for coming generations to learn how the power of lateral thinking and ingenuity, wedded with mathematical brilliance, an adventurous spirit of engineering, and inexhaustible optimism and energy in the face of a seemingly impossible challenge, helped bring about what essayist George Steiner termed 'one of the greatest achievements of the twentieth century'.

TO BE KEPT UNDER LOCK AND KEY AND NEVER TO BE REMOVED FROM THE OFFICE
THIS FORM IS TO BE USED FOR AIR INTELLIGENCE MESSAGES ONLY

174   BLETCHLEY PARK: THE SECRET ARCHIVES

LEFT The film's bar scenes, here featuring Keira Knightley as Joan Clarke, were filmed in the house's ballroom; the jolly atmosphere, if not the bar fittings, were a splendid echo of the room's rumbustious history.

BELOW Few would have taken the film as a scene-by-scene documentary; and countless viewers who have seen it either in the cinema or on DVD have been inspired to visit the Park to understand the reality.

OPPOSITE BOTTOM For purely dramatic reasons, the film focused on just the one bombe machine and wrote the Wrens out almost altogether. Some veterans were amused, others rather than alarmed, by the cinematic alterations.

ACKNOWLEDGEMENTS

First of all, with huge gratitude to the indefatigable
Kelsey Griffin, Bletchley Park's Director of Museum
Operations, who not only opened up a treasure
trove of rare pictures but was also extremely
generous with her time; Iain Standen, Bletchley
Park's CEO, who has been passed the baton and
is masterminding the coming stages of Bletchley's
full glorious regeneration; Sue May for endless
patience; plus Bletchley Park's team of dedicated
archivists and even more dedicated volunteers,
without whom the Park would really not be the
same. Thanks to Ian Allen for excellent editing
and to managing editor Melissa Smith for the
formidable job of pulling the entire thing together,
with a sharp eye and good humour. And not least
thanks to publishing director at Aurum, Graham
Coster, whose idea this was in the first place.

PICTURE CREDITS

The images included in this book are courtesy and
by permission of the following archives, collections
and libraries:

Bletchley Park Trust (with some contemporary
photos (c) shaunarmstrong/ mubsta.com) 2-3,
4 (all except second row, right), 10 (top and
bottom), 11 (left and right), 12 (top and bottom),
12-3, 14, 16, 18, 19, 20, 21, 22, 22-3, 24, 25, 37
(top and left), 38, 39, 40, 41, 44, 45, 54, 59, 65,
68, 69 – 74 (left), 75 (left), 77-9, 81, 84 (top), 85,
88, 122 (top, middle), 138, 139, 140-141, 141
(middle), 142, 146-7, 147, 148, 151, 152, 154, 155
(top), 156 (top), 158-9, 159-164 (bottom), 165,
166 (top left and bottom), 168-9, 169; U.S. Air
Force photo courtesy of Dr David Hamer (Enigma
decript) 4 (second row, right); English Heritage 6,
100, (Aerofilms Collection) 26-7. 31 (right), 80-1,
84 (bottom); The Centre for Buckinghamshire
Studies 13 (right), 16 (bottom), 17, (courtesy of
Dorothy Amelia Brown) 7, 74 (right); British Chess
Magazine 8 (left), 134 (bottom); Crown Copyright,
reproduced by permission Director GCHQ 8
(bottom), 28, 29, 30, 31 (bottom), 32, 33, 34, 36-
37, 56-7, 61, 110 (top), 126 (bottom), 145; City
of Westminster Archives Centre 9; The National
Archives UK 26, 35, 76, 125 (top), 130, 132; Getty
Images 64 (middle), 67 (left), 107, 199 (left), (SSPL)
32-33, 130-1, (Fox Photos) 51 (left), (Popperfoto)
81 (left), 82, 123 (right), 164 (top), (Fox Photos/
Hulton Archive) 89 (top), (Express) 105, 113 (top),
(Elliott & Fry/Hulton Archive) 106, 111 (bottom
right), (Carl Mydans/The LIFE Picture Collection)
112 (left), (Central Press) 114-5, 116, (George W.
Hales/Fox Photos) 117 (top), (DeAgostini) 118
(top), (ullstein bild) 118 (bottom), (Laski Diffusion)
119 (right), (Topical Press Agency) 120 (middle),
(The Print Collector) 124 (bottom right), (Paul
Popper/Popperfoto) 124 (bottom left), (Capt.
J L Evans/ IWM) 125 (centre), (PhotoQuest)
125 (bottom), (Daily Herald Archive/SSPL)
128-9, (Photo12/UIG) 129, (Evening Standard)
135 (bottom), (Chris Radburn/AFP) 166 (right),
(Eddie Mulholland - WPA Pool) 167, (LOCOG)
170; Rex Features (Ilpo Musto/Shutterstock) 37
(bottom right), 43 (bottom left and right), 171,
(Shutterstock/Associated Newspapers) 104 (top),
109, (Roger-Viollet) 122 (bottom), (Sonny Meddle)
148-9, 149, 153 (right), (Everett Collection)
150, (Andy Lauwers) 154 (bottom); Open
Library (tinyurl.com/offmgfj) 41; King's College
Archives, Cambridge 44 (bottom); Mary Evans
Picture Library 48, (Hildi Reinhart Collection)
46, (INTERFOTO / Heinrich Tannh‚user) 47;
Bedfordshire & Luton Archives Service 49; Press
Association Images 50, 103 (top), (Johnny Green),
153 (left); Topham Picturepoint (2000) 51 (top);

Reproduced by kind permission of His Grace the
Duke of Bedford and the Trustees of the Bedford
Estates 52; Alamy Stock Photo 104-5, 108, (: :
David Taylor Photography : :) 57 (top), 58 (middle),
(Maurice Savage) 57 (middle), 58 (top), (PCJones)
60 (left), (Prisma Bildagentur AG) 87, (David
Hunter) 120 (top), (Steve Vidler) 156 (bottom),
157; JAMES KING-HOLMES/BLETCHLEY
PARK TRUST/SCIENCE PHOTO LIBRARY 57
(bottom); Crypto Museum 63; Creative Commons
Attribution-ShareAlike License 65 (middle);
TopFoto (The Granger Collection) 68-9; Bob
Watt 75 (middle); Isabel Martin 75 (bottom);
By permission of Living Archive 81 (right), 83,
86 (bottom), 89 (bottom), 141 (bottom), 145
(bottom); Imperial War Museum (V151) 84
(middle), (A14494) 90, (IND4187) 90-1, (LD5765)
91, (A24959) 92 (top), (A10029) 92 (bottom),
(LD5765) 94-5, (GM1430) 96 (top), (A24959)
101, (A21428) 102 (left), (A14494) 102 (bottom),
(A7268) 115, (A12017) 120 (bottom), (A7268)
121 (top), (A21715) 121 (bottom), (E30918) 124
(top); Peter Budd 96 (bottom), 98, 99 (top left);
Ray Fautley 97 (top), 99 (bottom); Philip Nixon
(c) Copyright National Memorial Arboretum,
2012 103 (bottom); Mander and Mitchenson /
ArenaPAL 104 (bottom), 111 (top left); Supplied
by the Llyfrgell Genedlaethol Cymru/ National
Library of Wales 111 (bottom left); CORBIS
(Bettmann) 112 (left); National Archives, College
Park, MD, USA 113 (bottom right); St John's
College Cambridge tinyurl.com/qbz4yyy 117
(bottom), National Museums Scotland 122 (top
right and centre); Senior Common Room, Christ
Church Oxford 134 (top); School of Computer
Science, the University of Manchester 136
(bottom); Terri Pingilley (c) The Independent 137;
Chris Arnot 155 (bottom).

MEMORABILIA CREDITS

Item 1: (c) Mirrorpix
Items 2, 4, 5, 7, 8, 9, 11, 12, 13 and 15: (c) The
National Archives UK.
Item 10: (c) Public Record Office / HIP
Item 6: Courtesy of the Bletchley Park Trust
Items 3 and 14: Crown Copyright, reproduced by
permission of the Director GCHQ

STAFF CREDITS

Publisher: Richard Green
Senior Commissioning Editor: Jennifer Barr
Picture Research and Editorial Assistance: Daniela
Rogers
Layout and Design: Sooky Choi
Production: Rachel Ng and John Casey

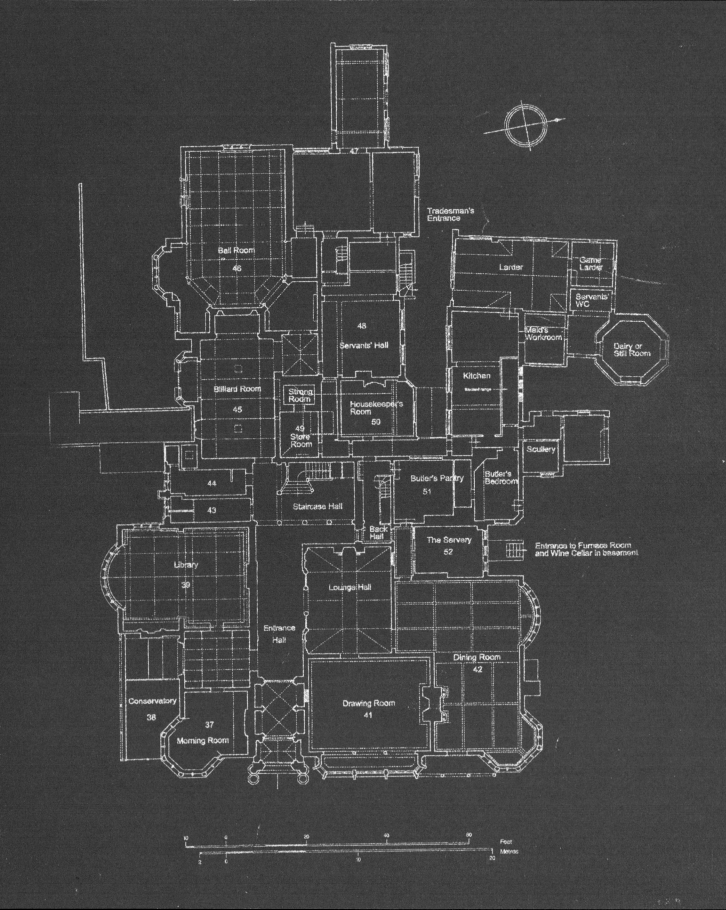